Ninja Foodi Smart XL Grill Cookbook 2020-2021

The Smart XL Grill That Sears, Sizzles, and Crisps. 6 in 1 Indoor Countertop Grill and Air Fryer Recipes for Your Whole Family

By Roger Kenzie

Copyright@2020-2021 by Roger Kenzie
All rights reserved worldwide.

No part of this book may be reproduced or transmitted in any form or by any means, electronic or mechanical, including photocopying, recording or by any information storage and retrieval system, without written permission from the publisher, except for the inclusion of brief quotations in a review.

Warning-Disclaimer
The purpose of this book is to educate and entertain. The author or publisher does not guarantee that anyone following the techniques, suggestions, tips, ideas, or strategies will become successful. The author and publisher shall have neither liability or responsibility to anyone with respect to any loss or damage caused, or alleged to be caused, directly or indirectly by the information contained in this book.

Contents

Introduction 10

    What is the Ninja Foodi Smart XL Grill? 11

    What are its Features and Functions? 11

    Tips for Getting Started 12

    Cooking Tips Tricks 13

    Care Maintenance Tips 14

Chapter No 1: 20 Grilled Recipes by Ninja Foodi Grill 16

    Delicious Donuts in Ninja Foodi Grill 16

    Frozen Barbecue Chicken Breasts 17

    Juicy Grilled Chicken Breasts 18

    Grilled Watermelon 19

    Ninja Foodi Grill Marinated Steak 20

    Ninja Foodi Grill Steak with Potatoes 21

    Grilled Pizza 22

    Grilled Cuban Pork Chops 23

    Grilled Plantains 24

    Cajun Seasoned Shrimp 25

    Grilled Salmon 26

    Orange Blossom Chicken 27

Ninja Foodi Ham Burger Pattie 28

Teriyaki Salmon 29

Smoked Ham Recipe..30

Grilled Broccoli 31

Grilled Chicken Legs in Ninja Foodi..32

Tri-Tip Roast in Ninja Foodi 33

Grilled Corn inside a Ninja Foodi..34

Strip Steak 35

Chapters No 2: Air Fried Recipes by Ninja Foodi Grill 36

Air Fryer Chicken Fajita Tacos... 36

Wings Recipe...37

Air Crisp Ninja Foodi Bacon Strips..38

Air Fryer Asparagus...39

Ninja Foodi French Fries..40

Air Fryer Rib-Eye Steak... 41

Air Fryer Steak Bites & Mushrooms...42

Crispy Air Fryer Zucchini Chips with Sriracha Aioli................................ 43

Air Fryer Ninja Foodi Eggplant..44

Breakfast Stuffed Peppers...45

 Crispy Air Fryer Chickpeas..46

Ninja Foodi Turkey Breast 47

Air Fryer Fries..48

Air Fryer Acorn Squash...49

Air Fried Teriyaki Chicken..50

Air Fryer Breakfast Frittata..51

Air Fryer Chicken Wings...52

Air Fryer Chicken Breast...53

Air-Fryer Eggplant Fries..54

Air Fried Lamb Chops..55

Chapter No 3: 20 Dehydrated Recipes by Ninja Foodi Grill.......56

Dehydrated Apples...56

Beef Jerky..57

Dehydrated Bananas..58

Dehydrated Watermelons..59

Dehydrated Zucchinis..60

Dehydrated Squash 61

Dehydrated Pineapple...62

Dehydrated Chili Pepper...63

Dehydrated Mangoes..64

Citrus Crisps...65

Dehydrated Thyme in Ninja Food..66

Dehydrated Rosemary in Ninja Foodi 67

Teriyaki Beef Turkey 68

Dehydrating Sweet Potato in Ninja Foodi 69

Dehydrated Potatoes Sticks.. 70

Dehydrated Plum Tomatoes... 71

Dehydrated Clementine's.. 72

Dehydrated Apricots.. 73

Beet Chips... 74

Dehydrated Mandarin Orange.. 75

Chapter No 4:20 Baked Recipes by Ninja Foodi Grill.................. 76

Baked Skillet Cookies in Ninja Foodi.. 76

Bake Potatoes in Ninja Foodi Grill.. 77

Ninja Foodi Baked Gluten-Free Oatmeal... 78

Baked Fish in Ninja Foodi... 79

Fish and Grits...80

Ninja Foodi Baked Pumpkin Oatmeal.. 81

Baked Western Omelets.. 82

Cheesy Egg Bake... 83

Mushroom and Egg Omelets... 84

Hash Brown... 85

Baked Salmon in Ninja Foodi Grill.. 86

Pound Cake in Ninja Foodi... 87

4 Ingredients Nutella Cake.. 88

Ninja Foodi Pumpkin Bread..89

Monkey Bread..90

Walnuts and Raspberries Cake 91

Ninja Foodi Lemon Cream Cheese Dump Cake 92

Ninja Foodi Apple Dump Cake 93

Chocolate Chip Cookie Cake 94

Baked Jerk Chicken 95

Chapter No 5:20 Roasted Recipes by Ninja Foodi Grill 96

Herbed Chicken 96

Lemon Chicken 97

Beef Chuck Roast with Root Vegetables 98

Ninja Foodi Pressure Cooker Pot Roast Recipe 99

Pork Roast 100

BBQ Ribs 101

Ninja Foodi Rosemary Roast and Potatoes 102

Ninja Foodi Roast Chicken 103

Ninja Foodi Prime Rib 104

Ninja Foodi Pot Roast 105

Roast Chicken in Ninja Foodi 106

Roasted Artichokes 107

Salmon with Apricot Sauce 108

Vegetable Egg Omelet 109

Roasted Chicken Drumsticks 110

Spaghetti Squash 111

Homemade Biscuits in Ninja Foodi...112

Blueberry Cake 113

Lemongrass and Coconut Chicken... 114

Roasted Cauliflower.. 115

Chapter No 6:21 Days Meal Plan.. 116

Week 1..117

Week 2..118

Week 3..119

Conclusion... 120

NINJA FOODI 6-IN-1 SMART XL GRILL FG551

FG551

NINJA Foodi SMART XL GRILL

- ✓ **6-qt. Capacity**
- ✓ **6 Functions**
- ✓ **Stainless Steel Finish**
- ✓ **15 Inspiration Recipe Guide Included**

Introduction

Indoor electric grills could easily be among everyone's favorite appliances of all time. Just imagine saying goodbye to the outdoors fuss and bringing the sunny grilling experience indoors not only during summer but all year round.

These kitchen gadgets come in two types: the contact grill and the open grill. The contact grill looks like a sandwich press that cooks food directly from two sides. The open grill, on the other hand, is similar to an electric griddle with ridges.

Indoor electric grills are not only popular during unfavorable weather conditions. These are also a big hit among those living in apartments and condominiums with limited space for grilling and entertaining a large group of visitors.

Using an indoor electric grill is also deemed safer and healthier as it eliminates the hazards of grilling outdoors, including burning coal, excessive smoke, and dripping fats.

With multifunctionality being a top trend in most kitchen gadgets in recent years, indoor electric grills can also do several things aside from yielding authentic char-grilled appearance, aroma, and taste in foods. Most indoor grills also function as another kitchen gadget craze—an air fryer.

One such versatile kitchen appliance is the Ninja Foodi Smart XL Grill.

What is the Ninja Foodi Smart XL Grill?

A 6-in-1 smokeless countertop grill, the Ninja Foodi Smart XL Grill can grill, air fry, bake, roast, broil and dehydrate foods. It comes with a 4-quart crisper basket and a 6-quart cooking pot. The air fry crisp function uses up to 75 percent less fat compared to deep frying.

Although this model cooks with its lid closed, only one side of food is in contact with the grill, making it an open grill type.

6 functions to elevate your cooking

- Grill
- Air Crisp
- Bake
- Roast
- Broil
- Dehydrate

What are its Features and Functions?

The Ninja Foodi Smart XL Grill features a Smart Cook System and a 500-degree Cyclonic Grilling Technology for evenly cooked results.

Forget about second-guessing whether the food is undercooked or overcooked. With the Smart Cook System, a touch of a button is all it takes to get rare to well-done meat with char-grilled marks and flavors. It features a dual-sensor Foodi Smart Thermometer, four smart settings for protein, and nine doneness levels.

The 1,760-watt Ninja Foodi Smart XL Grill also boasts a smoke control system that effectively keeps smoke out of the kitchen. Coupled with a cool-air zone, it has a splatter shield and a temperature-regulating grill grate.

Perfect for family-sized meals, the XL capacity of this model translates to 50 percent more food than the original Ninja Foodi Grill version. The 9-by-12 inches grill grate can fit up to six steaks, 24 hotdogs, or a main and side dishes at the same time.

Tips for Getting Started

Using electric grills and air fryers can be intimidating if you are operating them for the first time. Fear not because we have curated a few tips that any beginner user should know. Read on and let us get you grilling and more in no time.

Always prioritize safety and set aside time for reading the user manual that comes along with the Ninja Foodie Smart XL Grill first.

Electric grills may not look like it, but they usually get hot during and after use. Practice caution and use safety tools such as tongs and oven mitts when handling the device and the food.

Place the grill on a heat-proof surface, leaving at least 5 inches of space on all sides for sufficient airflow. Also, do not place it near water to avoid electric shocks.

Allow the device to preheat for a few minutes before adding the food. Preheating will allow the grill to reach the right temperature that will give you evenly cooked and beautifully char-grilled results. Preheating also avoids extended cooking time and food from sticking to the grate. Lightly grease the grill and basket even though they have nonstick coatings. Steer away, however, from aerosol cooking sprays as these can damage the device. We recommend getting a regular kitchen spray bottle filled with your choice of oil

Cooking Tips Tricks

The Ninja Foodi Smart XL Grill is practically like a convection oven. You can cook almost anything in it. You can use standard pans for baking with the air fryer function. From cakes and brownies to doughnuts and tarts-but keep an eye in case of the goods browning quickly.

You can also cook hard-boiled eggs directly in the air fryer. It would take about 15 minutes.

Try grilling vegetables such as broccoli wrapped in parchment paper. Doing so will give the vegetables the same texture from steaming, but with a hint of the charred flavor.

The air fryer is also perfect for toasting nuts. The cooking process will continue until after the nuts are unloaded from the fryer, so pull them out a bit earlier.

Frozen foods can also be cooked directly in your Ninja Foodi Smart XL Grill without thawing them first.

Say goodbye to bland and soggy leftovers-from roast chicken and salmon to pizza and vegetables. Reheat them in the air fryer for a crispier second time (or more) around.

Less is more when it comes to oil to achieve crispiness perfection. Grease too much, and you will get soggy instead of tasty evenly cooked crispy results. Neutral oils such as canola and vegetable oils are considered best for grilling because of their high smoking point. These also do not add unwanted flavor to the food.

Save the leftover fats in the pan for later to make pan sauces and gravies

Even with its size, make it a habit to cook in batches with your Ninja Foodi Smart XL Grill. Overcrowding food tends to obscure the hot air circulation inside, thereby affecting the crispiness and doneness of the food. Larger meats like pork chops, chicken cutlets, steaks, burgers, and fish fillets should be arranged in a single layer and not stacked one on top of the other.

Shaking the basket from time to time will also help to make sure everything inside the basket will cook and brown evenly.

Use the Foodi Smart Thermometer to check the doneness of meat accurately. Doing so not only helps to prevent overcooking but also ensures that the food is cooked enough and safe to eat.

Use oil to weigh down and glue your seasonings to the food. The air circulation inside the appliance may blow off lightweight particles such as spices while cooking. You can avoid this by mixing spices with oil before coating the food with them.

When cooking with marinated meats, let them sit on a cooling rack first to drain the excess liquids. Unlike outdoor grills, indoor grills do not drain liquid as well. So, doing this extra step will save you from cleaning marinades that dripped over your counter.

Care Maintenance Tips

A Ninja Foodi grill is a well-designed appliance, where the parts are removable and dishwasher safe. The best factor of the Ninja Foodi grill is that the control panel is easy to read as well. The maintenance as well as cleaning the appliance is easy. Grill preheats automatically but depends on settings. The shield can go into the dishwasher and can be cleaned easily. At the top of the lid lies a splatter shield that needed to be popped out after every cooking and needed to be cleaned as well.

The interior and exterior of the appliance did not get dirty very easily and can be clean regularly with wipe cleaner.

Chapter No 1: 20 Grilled Recipes by Ninja Foodi Grill

Delicious Donuts in Ninja Foodi Grill

Cooking Time: 10 Minutes
Yield: 6 Servings

Ingredients

1-1/2 cups sugar, powdered
1/3 cup whole milk
1/2 teaspoon vanilla extract
16 ounces of biscuit dough, prepared
Oil spray, for greasing
1 cup chocolate sprinkles, for sprinkling

Directions

Take a medium bowl and mix sugar, milk, and vanilla extract.
Combine well to create a glaze.
Set the glaze aside for further use.
Place the dough onto the flat clean surface.
Flat the dough with a rolling pin.
Use a ring mold, about an inch, and cut the hole in the center of each round dough.
Place the dough on a plate and refrigerate for 10 minutes.
Open the Ninja Foodi grill and install the grill grate inside it.
Close the hood.
Now, select the grill from the menu, and set the temperature to medium.
Set the time to 6 minutes.
Select start and begin preheating.
Remove the dough from the refrigerator and coat it with cooking spray from both sides.
When the unit beeps, the grill is preheated; place the adjustable amount of dough on the grill grate.
Close the hood, and cook for 3 minutes.
After 3 minutes, remove donuts and place the remaining dough inside.
Cook for 3 minutes.
Once, all the donuts are ready, sprinkle chocolate sprinkles on top.
Enjoy.
Remember to cool the donuts for 5 minutes before serving.

Nutrition Facts

Servings: 6
Amount per serving
Calories   400
% Daily Value*
Total Fat 11g 14%
Saturated Fat 4.2g   21%
Cholesterol 1mg   0%
Sodium 787mg   34%
Total Carbohydrate 71.3g 26%
Dietary Fiber 0.9g   3%
Total Sugars 45.3g
Protein 5.7g

Frozen Barbecue Chicken Breasts

Cooking Time: 20 Minutes
Yield: 4 Servings

Ingredients

4 frozen boneless, skinless chicken breasts (6-8 ounces each)
2 tablespoons canola oil, divided
Kosher salt, as desired
Ground black pepper, as desired
1 cup prepared barbecue sauce

Directions

The first step is to insert the grill grate inside the unit and close the hood.
Now, select the grill option and set the temperature to medium.
Set time to 20 minutes.
Now select start and begin the preheating process.
Meanwhile, brush each chicken piece with canola oil and season it with salt and black pepper.
Once the unit is preheated, place the chicken breast pieces onto the grill and close the hood.
Cook it for 8 minutes.
Then open the Ninja Foodi and flip the chicken and cook for 6 minutes.
Next, open the grill and baste the chicken with barbeque sauce from both the sides.
Continue cooking for 6 minutes.
Once done, remove the chicken from the unit and let it sit for 5 minutes before cutting and serving.
Enjoy.

Nutrition Facts

Servings: 4
Amount per serving
Calories 413
% Daily Value*
Total Fat 12.3g 16%
Saturated Fat 2g 10%
Cholesterol 131mg 44%
Sodium 845mg 37%
Total Carbohydrate 22.7g 8%
Dietary Fiber 0.4g 1%
Total Sugars 16.3g
Protein 49.3g

Juicy Grilled Chicken Breasts

Cooking Time: 17 Minutes
Yield: 4 Servings

Ingredients

4 chicken breasts, 8 ounces each
1/3 cup olive oil
3 tablespoon soy sauce
2 tablespoon balsamic vinegar
1/4 cup brown sugar
1 tablespoon Worcestershire sauce
3 tsp minced garlic
Salt and black pepper, to taste

Directions

Take a large bowl and whisk together soy sauce, vinegar, brown sugar, garlic, pepper, oil, salt, and Worcestershire sauce.
Take about cup of this mixture and set it aside for later serving.
Poke the chicken breast with a fork and soaked in the bowl marinate for 20 minutes.
Insert the grill grate to the unit and close the hood.
Now set the temperature to medium and set the timer to 10 minutes.
Once the grill is preheated, add chicken breast pieces into the grill and set the timer to 10 minutes.
After 5 minutes, open the unit and flip the chicken.
Cook for another 5 minutes.
After 5 minutes, baste the chicken with more basting liquid, cook for 2 minutes.
Once done, serve and enjoy.
Allow meat to rest for 5 minutes before cutting and serving.

Nutrition Facts

Servings: 4
Amount per serving
Calories   536
% Daily Value*
Total Fat 23.7g   30%
Saturated Fat 4.3g 22%
Cholesterol 175mg   58%
Sodium 864mg   38%
Total Carbohydrate 11.3g   4%
Dietary Fiber 0.2g   1%
Total Sugars 9.8g
Protein 66.6g

Grilled Watermelon

Cooking Time: 2 Minutes
Yield: 2-3 Servings

Ingredients

6 watermelon slices, each measuring 3 inches across and 1-inch thick
2 tablespoons honey

Directions

Put the grill grate inside the hood and close the unit.
Set temperature to the max and set the timer to 2 minutes.
Stop the unit as it is preheated.
Now brush the watermelon slices with honey.
Grease the grill grate with oil spray.
Place the watermelon slices on the grill grate.
Close the hood and grill for 2 minutes without flipping it.
Once done, take out watermelon slices and serve immediately.

Nutrition Facts

Servings: 2
Amount per serving
Calories   322
% Daily Value*
Total Fat 1.1g   1%
Saturated Fat 0.6g 3%
Cholesterol 0mg   0%
Sodium 12mg   1%
Total Carbohydrate 81.8g   30%
Dietary Fiber 3.4g 12%
Total Sugars 69.9g
Protein 5.1g

Ninja Foodi Grill Marinated Steak

Cooking Time: 8 Minutes
Yield: 2 Servings

Rare | 130-135 Degrees
Medium Rare | 140-145 Degrees
Medium | 155-160 Degrees
Well Done | 165 Degrees

Ingredients

12 ounces of Steak

Steak Marinade Ingredients

1/4 cup canola oil
3 cloves garlic, minced
1/4 teaspoon dried rosemary
1/3 teaspoon dried oregano
1/4 teaspoon dried thyme
1/4 teaspoon dried basil
Salt and black pepper, to taste

Directions

Mix all the marinade ingredients in a zip lock pack and put steak inside the zip lock pack
Marinate the steak in marinating liquid for 20 minutes.
Insert grill grate inside the Ninja Foodi grill and close the hood.
Preheat it for 10 minutes at Max.
Once preheated, the add food signal comes on display.
Open the grill and put the meat inside the grill.
Close the lid of the unit, and grill for 4-5 minutes.
Open and flip the steak and close the unit.
Grill for 4 more minutes.
Once done, serve and enjoy.

Nutrition Facts

Servings: 2
Amount per serving
Calories   588
% Daily Value*
Total Fat 35.8g   46%
Saturated Fat 5g   25%
Cholesterol 153mg   51%
Sodium 78mg   3%
Total Carbohydrate 1.9g 1%
Dietary Fiber 0.3g 1%
Total Sugars 0.1g
Protein 61.8g

Ninja Foodi Grill Steak with Potatoes

Cooking Time: 55 Minutes
Yield: 3 Servings

Ingredients

2 large russet potatoes, sliced in wedges
3 steaks, sirloin
1/4 cup of canola oil
2 tablespoons of steak seasoning
Salt, to taste

Directions

Wash and pat dry the potatoes.
Poke the potatoes with a fork.
Rub the canola oil on each of the potatoes and then sprinkle salt on top.
Put the potatoes into the air fryer basket and close the lid of the Ninja Foodi grill and set temperate to 400 degrees F.
Cook the potatoes for 30 minutes.
Once done, take out the potatoes and replace the air fryer basket with a grill grate.
Close the hood and set it to preheat for 10 minutes.
Now sprinkle steak with salt and steak seasoning.
Place the steak one at a time onto the grill grate and cook for 7-8 minutes in total.
Remember to flip to cook form another side after 4 minutes.
Once the steaks are done serve with potatoes.

Nutrition Facts

Servings: 3
Amount per serving
Calories   850
% Daily Value*
Total Fat 31.5g   40%
Saturated Fat 5.9g 29%
Cholesterol 235mg   78%
Sodium 183mg   8%
Total Carbohydrate 38.7g   14%
Dietary Fiber 5.9g 21%
Total Sugars 2.8g
Protein 98.4g

Grilled Pizza

Cooking Time: 10 Minutes
Yield: 4 Servings

Ingredients

2 tablespoons all-purpose flour, plus more as needed
6-8 ounces of pizza dough
1 tablespoon canola oil, divided
1/2 cup Alfredo sauce
1 cup mozzarella cheese, shredded
1/2 cup ricotta cheese, pieces
14 pepperoni slices
1/2 teaspoon of dried oregano for serving, optional

Directions

Place the grill grate inside the unit and close the hood.
Set temperatures to Max and let it preheat for 8 minutes.
Meanwhile, spread flour on a clean flat surface and roll the dough onto surface, using a rolling pin
Roll the dough and then cut in rod shape that it fits inside the grill grate.
Brush the dough evenly with canola oil and flip to coat the dough form another side as well.
Poke the dough with the fork.
Place it on the grill grate and close the hood.
Cook for 4 minutes and then flip to cook from another side by opening the hood.
Cook for 4 more minutes.
Now open the unit and spread sauce, cheeses, and pepperoni on top.
Close the hood and let it cook for 3 minutes.
Once it's done, serve with a sprinkle of oregano.

Nutrition Facts

Servings: 4
Amount per serving
Calories   465
% Daily Value*
Total Fat 31.6g   40%
Saturated Fat 10.3g   52%
Cholesterol 39mg 13%
Sodium 1335mg   58%
Total Carbohydrate 30.1g   11%
Dietary Fiber 1.6g 6%
Total Sugars 0.2g
Protein 15g

Grilled Cuban Pork Chops

Cooking Time: 7-8 Minutes
Yield: 4 Servings
Marinating Time 6 Hours

Ingredients

4 thick-cut pork chops
1/3 cup extra virgin olive oil
1/2 orange, zest only
1 cup orange juice * freshly squeezed
1 lime, zest
1 cup cilantro, finely chopped
1/4 cup mint leaves, chopped
4 cloves garlic, minced
2- Inch ginger, minced
2 teaspoons dried oregano
2 teaspoons ground cumin

Directions

Take a large mixing bowl and combine lime juice, lime zest, orange zest, olive oil, cilantro, oregano, cumin, ginger, and garlic.
Reserve about 1/4 cup of this marinade for further use.
Pour this marinates in a large mixing bowl and adds pork chops into the marinade for marinating.
Marinate the pork chop for 6 hours.
Now insert the grill grate into the Ninja Foodi grill and close the lid
Preheat at high temperature for 10 minutes.
Now after preheating the grill add pork chops to the grill grate and cook for about 7 minutes at medium heat.
After half time passes, open the unit and flip the chops to cook for another side.
Internal temperature should be 150 degrees F at the end of cooking.
Once done, serve.

Nutrition Facts

Servings: 4
Amount per serving
Calories   478
% Daily Value*
Total Fat 33.3g   43%
Saturated Fat 8.5g 42%
Cholesterol 80mg 27%
Sodium 267mg   12%
Total Carbohydrate 13.6g   5%
Dietary Fiber 2.2g 8%
Total Sugars 7.6g
Protein 35.5g

Grilled Plantains

Cooking Time: 6 Minutes
Yield: 2 Servings

Ingredients

2 Plantains, cut and sliced horizontally
1 tablespoon coconut oil, melted

Directions

Put the grill grate inside the Ninja Foodi grill and set the timer to 8 minutes at high for preheating.
Once, the grill is preheated, open the unit.
Brush the plantains with coconut oil and add to the hot grill.
Close the unit and cook for 3 minutes at medium.
Flip to cook from the other side and cook for an additional 3 minutes.
Once done, serve.

Nutrition Facts

Servings: 2
Amount per serving
Calories   277
% Daily Value*
Total Fat 7.5g   10%
Saturated Fat 6.1g 31%
Cholesterol 0mg   0%
Sodium 7mg   0%
Total Carbohydrate 57.1g   21%
Dietary Fiber 4.1g 15%
Total Sugars 26.9g
Protein 2.3g

Cajun Seasoned Shrimp

Cooking Time: 16-20 Minutes
Yield: 4 Servings
Ingredients

20 pieces of jumbo Shrimp
1/2 teaspoon of Cajun seasoning
1 tablespoon of Canola oil
1 teaspoon of magic shrimp seasoning

Directions

Take a large bowl and add canola oil, shrimp, and seasonings.
Mix well for fine coating.
Now put the shrimp on skewers.
Put the grill grate inside Ninja Foodi grill and set a timer to 8 minutes at high for preheating.
Once the grill is preheated, open the unit and place the shrimp skewers inside.
Cook the shrimp for 2 minutes.
Open the unit to flip the shrimp and cook for another 2 minutes at medium.
Own done, serve.

Nutrition Facts

Servings: 4
Amount per serving
Calories   382
% Daily Value*
Total Fat 7.4g   9%
Saturated Fat 0g   0%
Cholesterol 350mg   117%
Sodium 2208mg   96%
Total Carbohydrate 23.9g   9%
Dietary Fiber 2.6g 9%
Total Sugars 2.6g
Protein 50.2g

Grilled Salmon

Cooking Time: 7-14 Minutes
Yield: 4 Servings
Ingredients

4 fillets of salmon, 4 ounces each
Avocado oil spray
Seasoned salt, to taste
1 large lemon, juice only

Directions

First, spray the four fillets of salmon with avocado oil spray.
Now season the salmon fillets with seasoned salt and lemon juice.
Put the grill grate inside Ninja Foodi grill and set the timer to 8 minutes at high for preheating
Once the grill is preheated, open the unit.
Now place the salmon fillet inside the grill grate and cook at MAX for 7 minutes or until the internal temperate reaches 140 degrees.
Add fillet according to space inside the grill grate and do the cooking process in batch.
Once all the salmon is done serve and enjoy.

Nutrition Facts

Servings: 4
Amount per serving
Calories   277
% Daily Value*
Total Fat 12.1g   15%
Saturated Fat 3g   15%
Cholesterol 36mg   12%
Sodium 142mg   6%
Total Carbohydrate 1.4g 0%
Dietary Fiber 0.4g 2%
Total Sugars 0.4g
Protein 41.2g

Orange Blossom Chicken

Cooking Time: 12-24 Minutes
Yield: 4 Servings

Ingredients

2 tablespoons of orange zest
4 frozen boneless, skinless chicken breasts (8 ounces each)
2 tablespoons kosher salt
1 tablespoon sugar
1 tablespoon of avocado oil
1 cup cream
1 cup chicken broth
1 tablespoon instant flour

Directions

Insert the grill grate inside the unit and close the hood.
Now select the grill option and set the temperature to medium.
Set time to 20 minutes, for preheating.
Now select start and beginner preheating process.
Meanwhile, take a large bowl and mix chicken breast pieces with salt, sugar, almond flour, and orange zest.
Mix it well.
Add one tablespoon of avocado oil and rub the chicken well.
Once the preheating time complete and chicken is finely coated, place it on the grill grate.
Close the unit and cook for 6 minutes.
Then flip the chicken and cook for 7 minutes.
Once done remove the chicken from the unit and let it sit for 5 minutes before cutting and serving.
Serve and enjoy.

Nutrition Facts

Servings: 4
Amount per serving
Calories   417
% Daily Value*
Total Fat 11g   14%
Saturated Fat 4.2g 21%
Cholesterol 186mg   62%
Sodium 3842mg   167%
Total Carbohydrate 7.5g 3%
Dietary Fiber 0.5g 2%
Total Sugars 4.4g
Protein 67.7g

Ninja Foodi Ham Burger Pattie

Cooking Time: 9-18 Minutes
Yield: 3 Servings

Ingredients

2 cups of minced beef
1 large onion, grated
1 green chili, minced
1/3 teaspoon of ginger garlic paste
Salt and black pepper, to taste

Directions

Insert the grill grate inside the unit and close the hood.
Now select the grill option and set the temperature to medium.
Set time to 20 minutes, for preheating.
Take a large mixing bowl and then mix all the ingredients in it.
Make 4-inch patties of the meat.
Now open the unit once "add food" appears.
Put the patties inside the init and close the Ninja Foodi.
Cook for 9 minutes at 359 degrees F.
For great cooking experience, cook it in batches.
Once it's done, serve.

Nutrition Facts

Servings: 3
Amount per serving
Calories   656
% Daily Value*
Total Fat 21.3g   27%
Saturated Fat 8g   40%
Cholesterol 304mg   101%
Sodium 230mg   10%
Total Carbohydrate 5.3g 2%
Dietary Fiber 1.2g 4%
Total Sugars 2.4g
Protein 104g

Teriyaki Salmon

Cooking Time: 5 Minutes
Yield: 2 Servings

Ingredients

2 slices of salmon, skin on (4 ounces each)

Sauce Ingredients

1 tablespoon hoisin sauce
1 tablespoon soy sauce
1 tablespoon white vinegar
3 tablespoons sesame oil
1/4 cup packed light brown sugar
4 garlic cloves minced
1/2 teaspoon of ground ginger

Directions

Place the grill grate inside the unit and close it.
Preheat the grill by turning at high for 20 minutes.
Once it's preheated the "add food: on display will appear.
Meanwhile, prepare salmon.
First, mix all the sauce ingredients in a large bowl and transfer to a zip lock bag.
Place salmon inside the zip lock bag and mix well.
Place it in the refrigerator for 30 minutes.
Once marinated take out and place it on a grill grate and cook for 5 minutes at Max, skin side down.
Once done, serve.

Nutrition Facts

Servings: 2
Amount per serving
Calories   537
% Daily Value*
Total Fat 31.7g   41%
Saturated Fat 4.5g 23%
Cholesterol 79mg 26%
Sodium 214mg   9%
Total Carbohydrate 29.9g   11%
Dietary Fiber 0.4g 2%
Total Sugars 25.9g
Protein 35.3g

Smoked Ham Recipe

Cooking Time: 12-15 Minutes
Yield: 4 Servings

Ingredients

4 ounces of smoked ham, scored
1/2 cup of butter
2 tablespoons of brown sugar
1 tablespoon of honey
2 tablespoons of pineapple cane syrup

Directions

Place the grill rack inside the Ninja Foodi and pour a cup of water in it, then close the unit.
Let it preheat for 20 minutes at high.
Meanwhile melt butter in a cooking pot and add two tablespoons of brown sugar.
Melt it down and add a tablespoon of honey and pineapple cane syrup.
Mix well, and let it get simmer until thickened.
Turn off the Ninja Foodi and open the unit.
Then brush the ham with glaze.
Close the unit and cook for 7 minutes.
After 5 minutes open the unit by turning it off and glazed the ham again.
Cook for remaining 2 minutes
Sprinkle the ham with any favorite spice blend.
Slice and serve.

Nutrition Facts

Servings: 4
Amount per serving
Calories   291
% Daily Value*
Total Fat 25.5g   33%
Saturated Fat 15.4g   77%
Cholesterol 77mg 26%
Sodium 535mg   23%
Total Carbohydrate 12g 4%
Dietary Fiber 0.5g 2%
Total Sugars 10.7g
Protein 5g

Grilled Broccoli

Cooking Time: 3 Minutes
Yield: 1-2 Servings

Ingredients

2 cups of broccoli, fresh
1 tablespoon of canola oil
1 teaspoon of lemon pepper

Directions

Place the grill; grate inside the unit and close the hood.
Preheat the grill by turning at high for 10 minutes.
Meanwhile, mix broccoli with lemon pepper and canola oil.
Toss well to coat the ingredients well.
Place it on a grill grade once add food appears.
Lock the unit and cook for 3 minutes at medium.
Take out and serve.

Nutrition Facts

Servings: 2
Amount per serving
Calories   96
% Daily Value*
Total Fat 7.3g   9%
Saturated Fat 0.5g 3%
Cholesterol 0mg   0%
Sodium 30mg   1%
Total Carbohydrate 6.7g 2%
Dietary Fiber 2.7g   9%
Total Sugars 1.6g
Protein 2.7g

Grilled Chicken Legs in Ninja Foodi

Cooking Time: 20 minutes
Yield: 3 Servings

Ingredients

6 chicken legs
2 tablespoons of BBQ rubs
Canola oil spray

Directions

Take a plastic zip lock bag and spray it with canola oil.
Coat the legs with canola oil spray as well.
Add the legs to the zip lock bag and add the rub.
Shake it well for fine coating.
Preheat the Ninja Foodi for 10 minutes at 510 degrees.
Once add food option appears on display, place the legs inside the grill grate.
Close the unit and cook for 20 minutes at medium.
One half time pass, open the unit and Flip the less and then glazed the legs with BBQ sauce from both sides.
Close the unit and cook for 10 more minutes.
Once it's done serve.

Nutrition Facts

Servings: 3
Amount per serving
Calories   559
% Daily Value*
Total Fat 24.8g   32%
Saturated Fat 6.7g 34%
Cholesterol 274mg   91%
Sodium 512mg   22%
Total Carbohydrate 0g   0%
Dietary Fiber 0g   0%
Total Sugars 0g
Protein 78.9g

Tri-Tip Roast in Ninja Foodi

Cooking Time: 25minutes
Yield: 4 Servings
Ingredients

2 tablespoons of Beef rub and seasoning, victory lane beef rub
4 tablespoons of canola oil
2 pounds of tri-tip steak trimmed

Directions

Preheat the Ninja Foodi for about 10 minutes at 450 degrees.
Rub the meat with canola oil and then sprinkle rub on top.
Evenly coat the meat with oil spray and rub, and let it sit for 2 hours in the refrigerator.
Once the Ninja Foodi display read add food put the tri-tip inside the grill grade and close the unit.
Cook for 10 minutes at medium temperature.
Open the unit and flip the tri-tip.
Close the unit and cook for 15 more minutes.
After 10 minutes open the unit and flip to cook from the other side.
The internal temperatures should be 125 degrees.
Take out the steak and let it get cool.
Cut, slice and enjoy.
Enjoy.

Nutrition Facts

Servings: 4
Amount per serving
Calories 691
% Daily Value*
Total Fat 43.9g 56%
Saturated Fat 12.1g 60%
Cholesterol 152mg 51%
Sodium 193mg 8%
Total Carbohydrate 0g 0%
Dietary Fiber 0g 0%
Total Sugars 0g
Protein 69.6g

Grilled Corn inside a Ninja Foodi

Cooking Time: 10 Minutes
Yield: 4 Servings

Ingredients

4 corns
Avocado oil spray, for coating
1 cup of mayonnaise
1 cup sour cream
1 teaspoon of thyme, chopped
Salt and black pepper, to taste
6 tablespoons of lime juice

Directions

Insert grill grate inside the unit and preheat the unit for 10 minutes at 510 degrees MAX.
Meanwhile, coat the corn well with avocado oil.
Now make a sauce to glaze the corn.
Mix 1/4cup of mayonnaise and sour cream in a mixing bowl and mix well.
Add salt, black pepper, and freshly chopped thyme.
Add two tablespoons of lime juice.
Add in salt and black pepper.
Mix the ingredients well to make a delicious sauce.
Put the corn inside the grill grate.
Cover the unit and cook the corn for 10 minutes.
After 5 minutes of cooking, open the lid and flip the corn.
Cook for 5 more minutes.
Once done take out the corn and then let it sit on a cooling rack.
Drizzle generous amount of cream on top of the corn.
Use a brush to coat the corn well with the sauce.

Nutrition Facts

Servings: 4
Amount per serving
Calories   485
% Daily Value*
Total Fat 33.5g   43%
Saturated Fat 10.7g   53%
Cholesterol 41mg 14%
Sodium 471mg   20%
Total Carbohydrate 45.7g   17%
Dietary Fiber 4.3g 15%
Total Sugars 8.9g
Protein 7.4g

Strip Steak

Cooking Time: 10 Minutes
Yield: 2 Servings

Ingredients

Salt and black pepper
1/4 teaspoon of garlic powder
1.25 pounds of bone-in New York steak
Canola oil spray

Directions

Insert grill grate inside the unit and preheat the unit for 10 minutes, at 510 degrees MAX.
Rub the steak with salt, black pepper, and garlic powder.
Spray canola oil on both sides of the steak.
Place steak inside the grill grate and lower the hood.
Set time to 10 minutes, at 500 degrees F.
After 4 minutes open the lid and flip the steak to cook from other side.
Cook it for the remaining minutes.
Once done, take out and serve.

Nutrition Facts

Servings: 2
Amount per serving
Calories   581
% Daily Value*
Total Fat 38g   49%
Saturated Fat 15.1g   75%
Cholesterol 188mg   63%
Sodium 151mg   7%
Total Carbohydrate 0.3g 0%
Dietary Fiber 0g   0%
Total Sugars 0.1g
Protein 55.4g

Chapters No 2: Air Fried Recipes by Ninja Foodi Grill

Air Fryer Chicken Fajita Tacos

Cooking time: 20 minutes
Yield: 5 servings
Ingredients

2.5 pounds boneless, skinless chicken thighs
2 red bell peppers, diced
1/2 cup green bell pepper, diced
1/3 cup onion, diced
4 tablespoons taco seasoning
Olive oil spray/canola oil spray
10 flour tortillas

Directions

The first step is to spray the air fryer basket with canola oil spray.
Now, slice the chicken into desirable pieces.
Add onions, and bell peppers to the air fryer basket.
The coat he chickens with oil spray and then seasons it with taco seasoning.
Place chicken inside the air fryer basket.
Coat all the ingredients well with oil spray, inside the basket.
Cook at 390 degrees for 10 minutes, by pressing the air crisp.
Once 5 minutes pass, toss the ingredients inside the air fryer.
Take out the vegetables.
And spray oil the chicken again.
Cook for another 15 minutes.
Once the chicken is well done, serve it over warm tortillas with a topping of vegetables.

Nutrition Facts

Servings: 5
Amount per serving
Calories   573
% Daily Value*
Total Fat 18.3g   24%
Saturated Fat 4.9g 24%
Cholesterol 202mg   67%
Sodium 555mg   24%
Total Carbohydrate 29.6g   11%
Dietary Fiber 4.1g 15%
Total Sugars 4.3g
Protein 69g

Wings Recipe

Cooking Time: 25 Minutes
Yield: 3 Servings

Ingredients

1.5 pounds of chicken wings
1/4 teaspoon of Sea Salt
1/4 teaspoon of black pepper
1/2 teaspoon smoked paprika
1/2 teaspoon garlic powder
1/2 teaspoon onion powder
1 tablespoon of baking powder

Directions

In a mixing bowl add salt, black pepper, paprika, garlic powder, baking powder, and onion powder.
Add wings to the bowl and rub the wings generously with the spice mixture. Toss the wings for fine coating.
In the end, drizzle olive oil on top.
Use the air fryer crisp setting at 390 degrees.
Cook the wings in the air fryer inside Ninjas Foodi for 15 minutes.
Open the unit and flip the chicken and again cook for 5-10 minutes.
Serve the wings with your favorite sauce as side servings.

Nutrition Facts

Servings: 3
Amount per serving
Calories   440
% Daily Value*
Total Fat 16.9g   22%
Saturated Fat 4.6g 23%
Cholesterol 202mg   67%
Sodium 356mg   15%
Total Carbohydrate 3.3g 1%
Dietary Fiber 0.4g 1%
Total Sugars 0.3g
Protein 65.8g

Air Crisp Ninja Foodi Bacon Strips

Cooking Time: 15 Minutes
Yield: 2 Servings

Ingredients

1 cup of Bacon slices

Directions

Place bacon slices inside air fryer crisp. Set temperature to 360 F and cook the bacon for 15 minutes.
Once desire crispness obtained, serve and enjoy.

Nutrition Facts

Servings: 2
Amount per serving
Calories 40
% Daily Value*
Total Fat 3.5g 4%
Saturated Fat 1.3g 6%
Cholesterol 8mg 3%
Sodium 130mg 6%
Total Carbohydrate 0g 0%
Dietary Fiber 0g 0%
Total Sugars 0g
Protein 2.5g

Air Fryer Asparagus

Cooking Time: 7 Minutes
Yield: 2 Servings

Ingredients

1 pound of Asparagus
3 tablespoons of canola oil
Salt and black pepper, to taste

Directions

Wash, rinse, and pat dry the asparagus.
Beak the ends where the woody part starts.
Break from the part where asparagus naturally bents.
Place asparagus in the air fryer basket.
Don't overcrowd the basket.
Sprinkle salt, black pepper and drizzle canola oil on top.
Cook at 375 degrees for 10 minutes.
Cook the asparagus in batches.
Once it's done serve.

Nutrition Facts

Servings: 2
Amount per serving
Calories   231
% Daily Value*
Total Fat 21.3g   27%
Saturated Fat 1.6g 8%
Cholesterol 0mg   0%
Sodium 5mg   0%
Total Carbohydrate 8.8g 3%
Dietary Fiber 4.8g   17%
Total Sugars 4.3g
Protein 5g

Ninja Foodi French Fries

Cooking Time: 25 Minutes
Yield: 3 Servings

Servings: 3
Amount per serving
Calories   289
% Daily Value*
Total Fat 14g   18%
Saturated Fat 2g   10%
Cholesterol 0mg   0%
Sodium 63mg   3%
Total Carbohydrate 39.8g   14%
Dietary Fiber 3.1g   11%
Total Sugars 1.5g
Protein 4.6g

Ingredients

1.5 pounds of medium potatoes russet
3 tablespoons of olive oil
Seasoned salt, to taste

Directions

Slice the potatoes in a strip-like French fries.
Leave on the skin.
Rub the French fries with olive oil.
Season its salt.
Close the lid and cook for 20 minutes at 340 degrees by pressing the air crisp.
If you need it much brown then cook for a few more minutes.
Serve and enjoy.

Nutrition Facts

Air Fryer Rib-Eye Steak

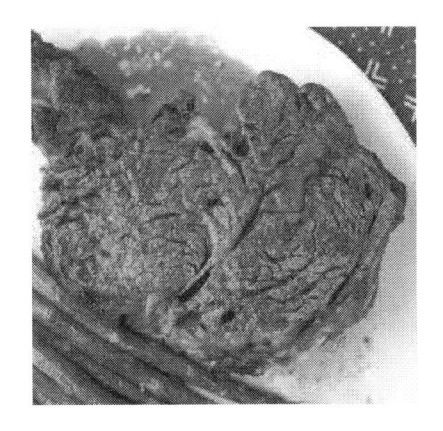

Cooking Time: 18 Minutes
Yield: 2 Servings

Ingredients

2 steaks rib-eye steaks
8 strips bacon
1 tablespoon of seasoned salt
1/3 teaspoon of chili powder
Black pepper, to taste
1 teaspoon garlic powder
1/2 teaspoon of onion powder

Directions

Preheat your air fryer at 375 degrees for 15 minutes.
Meanwhile, Mix all the seasoning in a bowl.
Put the steak on a cutting board and then rub it with a generous amount of seasoning.
Flip and rub the other part of the steak as well.
Wrap each steak with 4 pieces of bacon.
Place steak inside the air fryer basket and cook for 18-20 minutes.
Once half time pass, open Ninja Foodi and flip the steak.
Let it cook from the other side.
Once the steak is crisp, put it on a plate.
Serve after 5 minutes of cooling.

Nutrition Facts

Servings: 2
Amount per serving
Calories   558
% Daily Value*
Total Fat 43.1g   55%
Saturated Fat 12g 60%
Cholesterol 75mg 25%
Sodium 3230mg   140%
Total Carbohydrate 9.8g 4%
Dietary Fiber 4.3g 15%
Total Sugars 0.6g
Protein 28.4g

Air Fryer Steak Bites & Mushrooms

Cooking Time: 23 Minutes
Yield: 2 Servings

Ingredients

1 pound steak, cut into pieces
8 oz. mushrooms (cleaned, washed)
4 tablespoons of butter, Melted
2 teaspoons of Worcestershire sauce
Red chili flakes, optional
1 teaspoon of garlic powder
Salt and black pepper, to taste

Directions

Preheat the Air Fryer at 400°F for 5 minutes.
Meanwhile, rinse and pat dry the steak. In a large mixing bowl, mix steak and mushroom.
Coat the steak and mushroom with melted butter and season it with garlic powder, and Worcestershire sauce
In the end, add seasoning of salt and black pepper.
Place the mushroom and steak mixture inside the air fryer.
Cook it for 10 minutes at 400 degrees.
Then flip the ingredients and cook for 10 more minutes.
You can cook it for an extra 2 to 3 minutes to achieve the desired texture.
Serve it with a drizzle of butter and red chili flakes.
Serve warm and enjoy.

Nutrition Facts

Servings: 2
Amount per serving
Calories   689
% Daily Value*
Total Fat 34.7g   45%
Saturated Fat 18.5g   92%
Cholesterol 265mg   88%
Sodium 328mg   14%
Total Carbohydrate 5.8g 2%
Dietary Fiber 1.3g 5%
Total Sugars 3.3g
Protein 86g

Crispy Air Fryer Zucchini Chips with Sriracha Aioli

Cooking Time: 12 Minutes
Yield: 4 Servings

Ingredients

16 slices of zucchini (skin on), cut 1/16 inch thick
1/4 cup flour, for coating
1 large egg
1/2 cup Panko bread crumbs
Salt, to taste
Garlic powder, to taste
Black pepper, to taste
1/4 teaspoon of cayenne pepper
Red chili flakes, to taste

Sriracha Aioli ingredient

1/3 Cup mayonnaise
1 teaspoon or more of Sriracha

Directions

Slice the zucchinis into thick round shapes.
Place the zucchinis in a bowl and add salt, pepper, garlic powder, Panko.
Mix well for fine coating.
Add cayenne and red pepper as well for a spicy kick.
Put flour in a separate bowl as well.
Beat the egg in a separate bowl.
First, dredge the zucchini in flour then in egg and at last Panko mix.
Shake off excess, and place in the fryer basket.
Set the temperature to 390 degrees and set the timer for 12 minutes.
Cook it in batches.
Mix the sauce ingredients in a bowl.
Once all zucchini is done, serve with a bowl.
Enjoy.

Nutrition Facts

Servings: 4
Amount per serving
Calories   183
% Daily Value*
Total Fat 8.7g   11%
Saturated Fat 1.5g 8%
Cholesterol 52mg   17%
Sodium 298mg   13%
Total Carbohydrate 21.9g   8%
Dietary Fiber 1.3g 5%
Total Sugars 2.9g
Protein 4.9g

Air Fryer Ninja Foodi Eggplant

Cooking Time: 20 Minutes
Yield: 2 Servings

Ingredients

2 large eggplants
3 eggs beaten
1/3 cup Panko breadcrumbs
1 cup mozzarella cheese
2 cups of marinara sauce
Olive oil spray

Directions

Peel and slice the eggplants.
Take a shallow bowl and then place bread crumbs in it.
Take a small bowl and scramble eggs in it.
Dip the eggplants first in the egg mixture and then dip it into bread crumbs.
Preheat the Ninja Foodi for 5 minutes.
Spray the inner basket with canola oil spray.
Put eggplants inside and close the unit.
Select the air crisp option and adjust temperate to 400 degrees f.
Set timer to 16 minutes.
After 12 minutes open the unit and brush it with oil.
Cook for reaming 4 minutes.
Lay the slices of eggplants with mozzarella cheese.
Close the lid and select broil for few mints about 2 – 4 minutes.
Then serve with marinara sauce.

Nutrition Facts

Servings: 2
Amount per serving
Calories   570
% Daily Value*
Total Fat 19g   24%
Saturated Fat 6.2g 31%
Cholesterol 292mg   97%
Sodium 1227mg   53%
Total Carbohydrate 70.4g   26%
Dietary Fiber 25.9g 93%
Total Sugars 39.5g
Protein 23.8g

Breakfast Stuffed Peppers

Cooking Time: 14 Minutes
Yield: 2 Servings

Ingredients

2 bell pepper halved, middle seeds removed
4 eggs
2 teaspoons of olive oil
Salt and pepper, to taste
Sriracha flakes, to taste

Directions

Cut the bell pepper lengthwise and then remove all the seeds.
Rub olive oil all over the bell peppers.
Crack eggs into each bell pepper holes and sprinkle salt, Sriracha flakes, and black pepper.
Now place the bell pepper inside the Ninja Foodi and lock the lid.
Turn on the unit and set temperature rot 360 degrees F for 14 minutes.
Once the time pass and eggs get cooked take out the bell peppers.
Serve and enjoy.

Nutrition Facts

Servings: 2
Amount per serving
Calories   190
% Daily Value*
Total Fat 13.6g   17%
Saturated Fat 3.4g 17%
Cholesterol 327mg   109%
Sodium 126mg   5%
Total Carbohydrate 6.2g 2%
Dietary Fiber 2g   7%
Total Sugars 3.5g
Protein 12.1g

Crispy Air Fryer Chickpeas

Cooking Time: 15 Minutes
Yield: 3 Servings

Ingredients

16 ounces Of Chickpeas, drained and rinsed
1 tablespoon Olive Oil
1-ounce Packet Ranch Salad Dressing & Seasoning Mix
3 tablespoons Parmesan Cheese

Directions

Heat the Ninja Foodi air fryer at 390 degrees for 10 minutes.
Drain and rinse the chickpeas in a bowl, and then toss in one tablespoon of olive oil.
Toss parmesan cheese and ranch seasoning as well.
Mix all the ingredients well
Now pour the chicken peas into the air fryer basket.
Let it cook for 15 minutes.
Remember to shake the chickpeas in between.
When the chickpeas are crisp, remove them from the basket.
Store in an airtight container or serve.
Enjoy.

Ninja Foodi Turkey Breast

Cooking Time: 30 Minutes
Yield: 4 Servings

Ingredients

2.5-pound boneless turkey breast, thawed
1/3 tablespoons of rosemary
Salt and black pepper, to taste
1 tablespoon of olive oil
Olive oil spray

Directions

Place the turkey breast inside the Ninja Foodi air fryer basket.
Coat the breast with olive oil, salt, pepper, and rosemary.
Turn the breast and coat it generously with oil, salt, pepper and rosemary from the other side.
Close the lid and cook for 30 minutes at 350 by turning on the air fry option.
Flip the breast after 15 minutes by opening the unit.
Once cooking is done, let it rest and then serve.
Enjoy by slicing into pieces.

Nutrition Facts

Servings: 4
Amount per serving
Calories   307
% Daily Value*
Total Fat 4.8g   6%
Saturated Fat 0.5g 3%
Cholesterol 176mg   59%
Sodium 138mg   6%
Total Carbohydrate 0.2g 0%
Dietary Fiber 0.1g 0%
Total Sugars 0g
Protein 70.3g

Air Fryer Fries

Nutrition Facts

Servings: 2
Amount per serving
Calories   797
% Daily Value*
Total Fat 34.3g   44%
Saturated Fat 5g   25%
Cholesterol 0mg   0%
Sodium 44mg   2%
Total Carbohydrate 115.9g   42%
Dietary Fiber 17.7g 63%
Total Sugars 8.5g
Protein 12.4g

Cooking Time: 20minutes
Yield: 2 Servings

Ingredients

4 large russet potatoes
1/3 cup of olive oil

Directions

Cut the potatoes into wedges according to the desired thickness.
Mix all the remaining ingredients in a bowl and toss wedges in it.
Pour water inside the bottom of the air fryer basket.
Then place an air fryer basket on top. Lock the unit and cook for 20 minutes at 400 degrees F.
Once done, serve and remove.

Air Fryer Acorn Squash

Cooking Time: 15 minutes
Yield: 2 Servings

Ingredients

2 acorn squash
2 tablespoons of avocado oil
2 teaspoons of poultry seasoning
Seasoned salt, to taste
Black pepper, to taste

Directions

Cut the vegetable down the middle lengthwise.
Scrap the seeds and discard them.
Scrap out the seeds and cut the acorn squash into thick slices.
Take a mixing bowl and toss together squash, Oil, seasoning, seasoned salt, and pepper,
Mix well.
Place the vegetables in the air fryer basket.
Turn on the air fryer by pressing air crisp.
Cook it for 15 minutes at 385 degrees.
Once done, serve.

Nutrition Facts

Servings: 2
Amount per serving
Calories   196
% Daily Value*
Total Fat 2.3g   3%
Saturated Fat 0.5g 3%
Cholesterol 0mg   0%
Sodium 109mg   5%
Total Carbohydrate 46.7g   17%
Dietary Fiber 7.3g 26%
Total Sugars 0.1g
Protein 3.8g

Air Fried Teriyaki Chicken

Cooking Time: 22 Minutes
Yield: 3 Servings

Ingredients

6 drum stick, chicken
1/3 cup of soy sauce
1/4 cup of maple syrup
1/3 cup of brown sugar
1/3 cup of rice wine vinegar
4 cloves of garlic
1 inch of ginger garlic paste
Red chili flakes, to taste
Salt and black pepper, to taste
2 cups of water

Directions

Place all the ingredients in a zip lock bag and mix well so the drumsticks are coated well with the marinade.
Squeeze all the air out form the zip lock bag.
Marinate the chicken for a few hours in the refrigerator.
Drain the marinade liquid and then add the chicken to the air fryer basket.
Set temperature to 400 degrees and cook for 22 minutes.
Once done, serve.

Nutrition Facts

Servings: 3
Amount per serving
Calories   591
% Daily Value*
Total Fat 24.1g   31%
Saturated Fat 6.6g 33%
Cholesterol 244mg   81%
Sodium 1885mg   82%
Total Carbohydrate 37.1g   13%
Dietary Fiber 0.3g 1%
Total Sugars 31.8g
Protein 48.1g

Air Fryer Breakfast Frittata

Cooking Time: 20 Minutes
Yield: 1 Serving

Ingredients

1/2 pounds of sausage, breakfast sausage
3 -5 eggs, beaten
1/2 cup Monterey jack cheese
4 tablespoons of bell pepper
1 green onion
1 pinch of cayenne pepper, or to taste

Directions

Mix eggs, sausage, cheese, bell pepper, onion, and cayenne pepper in a large mixing bowl and combine well.
Preheat the air fryer to 350 degrees for 10 minutes.
Spray the basket with oil spray and then pour the mixture inside it.
Cook it inside the air fryer for 20 minutes. Once done, serve and enjoy.

Nutrition Facts

Servings: 1
Amount per serving
Calories   1325
% Daily Value*
Total Fat 95.8g   123%
Saturated Fat 35.6g   178%
Cholesterol 732mg   244%
Sodium 2201mg   96%
Total Carbohydrate 38.5g   14%
Dietary Fiber 6.8g   24%
Total Sugars 25.7g
Protein 79.6g

Air Fryer Chicken Wings

Cooking Time: 2-4 Minutes
Yield: 4 Servings

Ingredients

Cooking spray for greasing
2 pounds of chicken wings
Salt and black pepper, to taste
6 tablespoons of butter
1/3 cup of hot sauce
1/4 cup of Ranch cheese, or per liking

Directions

Spray the air fryer basket with cooking spray.
Rub the chicken pieces with salt, black pepper and place the wings inside the basket.
Turn on the Ninja Foodi and press air crisp.
Set temperature to 400 degrees for 20 minutes.
Meanwhile melt butter in a pan and add hot sauce.
Once done, take out wings and glaze it with hot sauce.
And serve with the topping of cheese.
Enjoy.

Nutrition Facts

Servings: 4
Amount per serving
Calories   767
% Daily Value*
Total Fat 50.8g   65%
Saturated Fat 22.4g   112%
Cholesterol 285mg   95%
Sodium 1245mg   54%
Total Carbohydrate 1.9g 1%
Dietary Fiber 0.1g 0%
Total Sugars 1.8g
Protein 73.4g

Air Fryer Chicken Breast

Nutrition Facts

Servings: 3
Amount per serving
Calories   467
% Daily Value*
Total Fat 18.2g   23%
Saturated Fat 5g   25%
Cholesterol 219mg   73%
Sodium 211mg   9%
Total Carbohydrate 0g   0%
Dietary Fiber 0g   0%
Total Sugars 0g
Protein 71.1g

Cooking Time: 25 Minutes
Yield: 3 Servings
Ingredients

26 ounces of chicken breasts
Salt and Black pepper, to taste
1-2 teaspoons of Chili lime Trader Joe seasoning

Directions

Slice the chicken breast in half and season it with salt, trade Joe chili lime seasoning and, black pepper.
Turn on the Ninja Foodi and press air crisp.
Set the timer to 25 minutes at 400 degrees F.
Once the chicken is done and the timer is accepted, take out and serve.

Air-Fryer Eggplant Fries

Cooking Time: 7 Minutes
Yield: 3 Servings

Ingredients

3 large eggplants
1/3 cup grated Parmesan cheese
1/3 cup toasted wheat germ
2 teaspoons Italian seasoning
1/4 teaspoon garlic salt
1 cup meatless pasta sauce, warmed
Oil spray for cooking

Directions

Preheat the air fryer to 400 degrees F.
Cut the eggplants into slices.
Oil sprays the eggplant slices.
Mix cheese, wheat germ, Italian seasoning, and garlic salt in a bowl.
Whisk egg in a mixing bowl.
Dip eggplant first in egg and then coat with cheese mixture.
Coat the air fryer basket with cooking spray and place eggplant slices inside it
Cook until golden brown, 5-7 minutes.
Turn eggplant halfway through.
Continue cooking until golden brown, 4-5 minutes.
Once done, serve with pasta dipping sauce.

Nutrition Facts

Servings: 3
Amount per serving
Calories   359
% Daily Value*
Total Fat 11.7g   15%
Saturated Fat 5g   25%
Cholesterol 24mg 8%
Sodium 614mg   27%
Total Carbohydrate 51.4g   19%
Dietary Fiber 23.4g 84%
Total Sugars 25.1g
Protein 19.6g

Air Fried Lamb Chops

Cooking Time: 5 Minutes
Yield: 3 Servings

Ingredients

2.5 pounds of lamb chops
Salt and black pepper, to taste
1/2 cup Greek yogurt
4 tablespoons of honey
Cayenne pepper, to taste

Directions

Cut the lamb chop into individual pieces to make individual lamb chop.
Season the chop with salt, black pepper.
Rub generous for fine coating.
Now rub the chops with cayenne pepper.
Drizzle honey over the lamb and baste it with a brush from both sides.
Season the lamb chops from both sides.
Now brush the chop with geek yogurt from both sided.
Now coat their fryer basket with oil spray.
Press air crisp and set the temperature at 450 degrees and set a timer for 10 minutes for preheating.
Press start and let the Ninja Foodi preheated.
Now layer air crisp liner inside air crisp basket.
And place lamb chop in the basket, and cook for 5 minutes inside the unit once preheating is done.
Once done, open Ninja Foodi and take out lamb chops.

Nutrition Facts

Servings: 3
Amount per serving
Calories   940
% Daily Value*
Total Fat 31.8g   41%
Saturated Fat 12.9g   65%
Cholesterol 350mg   117%
Sodium 354mg   15%
Total Carbohydrate 31.2g   11%
Dietary Fiber 0.1g 0%
Total Sugars 31.1g
Protein 126.4g

Chapter No 3: 20 Dehydrated Recipes by Ninja Foodi Grill

Dehydrated Apples

Cooking Time: 5- 6hours
Yield: 3 Servings

Ingredients

5 small apples peeled, cored, sliced thin
1/4 cup cinnamon
4 tablespoons of sugar

Directions

Core and peel the apples.
Take a mandolin to cut the apples into slices.
Mix cinnamon and sugar in a bowl and shake apple slices in it.
Place the apples in the rack and sprinkle reaming cinnamon and sugar over the apples.
Close the unit and dehydrate the apples at 145 degrees for 6 hours. Check at 5-hour intervals and keep in for a longer time for desired crispness. Enjoy.

Nutrition Facts

Servings: 3
Amount per serving
Calories   214
% Daily Value*
Total Fat 0.1g   0%
Saturated Fat 0g   0%
Cholesterol 0mg   0%
Sodium 1mg   0%
Total Carbohydrate 59.6g   22%
Dietary Fiber 13.1g 47%
Total Sugars 44.2g
Protein 0.4g

Beef Jerky

Cooking Time: 7 Hours
Yield: 6 Servings

Ingredients

1/4 cup soy sauce
2 tablespoons Worcestershire sauce
2 tablespoons dark brown sugar
1 teaspoon ground black pepper
1 teaspoon garlic powder
1 teaspoon onion powder
1 teaspoon paprika
2 teaspoons kosher salt
1 1/2 pounds uncooked beef eye of round, cut in 1/4-inch slices

Directions

Take a large bowl and mix soy sauce, Worcestershire sauce, black pepper, garlic powder, and onion powder, paprika, salt, and dark brown sugar. Place all these ingredients in a zip lock bag.

Place the slices of beef in a bag and mix well.

Let it marinate for 4 hours in the refrigerator.

Now take out the meat and strain excess liquid.

Layer the meat on a Ninja dehydrator rack.

Press the DEHYDRATE, set the temperature to 155 degrees F, and set time to 7 hours.

When cooking is complete, remove jerky from the dehydrating rack and serve after cooling.

Nutrition Facts

Servings: 6
Amount per serving
Calories   52
% Daily Value*
Total Fat 0.8g   1%
Saturated Fat 0.3g 1%
Cholesterol 10mg 3%
Sodium 1440mg   63%
Total Carbohydrate 5.8g 2%
Dietary Fiber 0.4g 1%
Total Sugars 4.4g
Protein 5.3g

Dehydrated Bananas

Cooking Time: 10 Hours
Yield: 2 Servings

Ingredients

4 bananas, peeled and sliced
Few tablespoons for orange juice

Directions

Layer bananas inside hate Ninja Foodi rack and lightly coat it with orange juice.
Now press the dehydrate button and adjust the time to 10 hours.
Open the lid and then take out the bananas.
Serve.

Nutrition Facts

Servings: 2
Amount per serving
Calories   217
% Daily Value*

Total Fat 0.8g   1%
Saturated Fat 0.3g 1%
Cholesterol 0mg   0%
Sodium 2mg   0%
Total Carbohydrate 55.5g   20%
Dietary Fiber 6.2g 22%
Total Sugars 30.2g
Protein 2.7g

Dehydrated Watermelons

Cooking Time: 7 Hours
Yield: 4 Servings

Ingredients

2 pounds of Watermelon, peeled and cut into wedges

Directions

First cut the watermelon into thin wedges.
Layer the slices of watermelon on multiple dehydration rack.
Remember to coat the rack with oil spray so the chips do not stick to the rack.
Place the rack inside the Ninja Foodi and then close the unit.
Turn on the Ninja Foodi and press the dehydrate button and Set a time to 7 hours at 130 degrees F.
Once time complete open the unit and serve

Nutrition Facts

Servings: 4
Amount per serving
Calories   68
% Daily Value*
Total Fat 0.3g   0%
Saturated Fat 0.2g 1%
Cholesterol 0mg   0%
Sodium 3mg   0%
Total Carbohydrate 17g 6%
Dietary Fiber 0.9g 3%
Total Sugars 13.9g
Protein 1.3g

Dehydrated Zucchinis

Cooking Time: 7 Hours
Yield: 1 Serving

Ingredients

2 zucchinis, large
1 teaspoon of seasoned salt

Directions

Cut the zucchinis into thin round slices.
Season it with seasoned salt.
Layer the zucchini on to dehydrator racks.
Remember to coat the rack with oil spray so the chips do not stick to the rack.
Put the slices inside the Ninja Foodi and then turn on the unit.
Now place the rack inside the Ninja Foodi and set timer at 135 degrees for 7 hours.
Once done, serve and enjoy.

Nutrition Facts

Servings: 1
Amount per serving
Calories   63
% Daily Value*
Total Fat 0.7g   1%
Saturated Fat 0.2g 1%
Cholesterol 0mg   0%
Sodium 1559mg   68%
Total Carbohydrate 13.1g   5%
Dietary Fiber 4.3g   15%
Total Sugars 6.8g
Protein 4.7g

Dehydrated Squash

Cooking Time: 7 Hours
Yield: 2 Servings

Ingredients

2 cups yellow summer squash, large
Seasoned salt
Paprika

Directions

Cut the squash into round thin slices
Layer the slices on to dehydrator racks. Remember to coat the rack with oil spray so the chips do not stick to the rack.
Put it inside the Ninja Foodi and then turn on the unit.
Sprinkle some seasoned salt on top.
Set the timer at 135 degrees for 7 hours
Once done takeout chips and serve.

Nutrition Facts

Servings: 2
Amount per serving
Calories   24
% Daily Value*
Total Fat 0.3g   0%
Saturated Fat 0.1g 1%
Cholesterol 0mg   0%
Sodium 3mg   0%
Total Carbohydrate 4.9g 2%
Dietary Fiber 1.3g 5%
Total Sugars 4.5g
Protein 1.3g

Dehydrated Pineapple

Servings: 4
Amount per serving
Calories   41
% Daily Value*
Total Fat 0.1g   0%
Saturated Fat 0g   0%
Cholesterol 0mg   0%
Sodium 1mg   0%
Total Carbohydrate 10.8g   4%
Dietary Fiber 1.2g   4%
Total Sugars 8.1g
Protein 0.4g

Cooking Time: 8 Hours
Yield: 4 Servings

Ingredients

2 cups of pineapples, drained
Oil spray, for greasing
Salt, pinch

Directions

Take dehydrating rack and coat it with oil spray.
Layer all the round pineapples onto the racks.
Place the rack it inside the Ninja Foodi and then turn on the unit.
The set timer at 135 degrees for 8 hours.
Once done takeout the chips and serve.
Nutrition Facts

Dehydrated Chili Pepper

Total Fat 0.4g   1%
Saturated Fat 0.1g 0%
Cholesterol 0mg   0%
Sodium 6mg   0%
Total Carbohydrate 5.5g 2%
Dietary Fiber 2g   7%
Total Sugars 3.2g
Protein 0.9g

Cooking Time: 6 Hours
Yield: 2 cups

1 cup green chilies pepper, slices
1 cup red chili peppers

Directions

Take a stainless steel rack and layer red and green chili peppers onto the rack.
Put the rack inside Ninja Foodi.
Set dehydrator to 135 degrees F and set the timer to 6 hours.
One time complete takeout the chili pepper.
Reserve in an airtight glass jar or use it as needed.

Nutrition Facts

Servings: 6
Amount per serving
Calories   25
% Daily Value*

Dehydrated Mangoes

Amount per serving
Calories 396
% Daily Value*
Total Fat 2.5g 3%
Saturated Fat 0.6g 3%
Cholesterol 0mg 0%
Sodium 7mg 0%
Total Carbohydrate 98.9g 36%
Dietary Fiber 10.6g 38%
Total Sugars 90.2g
Protein 5.4g

Cooking Time: 6 hours
Yield: 4 Servings

Ingredients

16 slices mangos, thin cut

Directions

Take dehydrating racks and spray it with canola oil.
Wash and peel the mangoes lengthwise.
Layer the slices on the rack.
Place the rack inside the Ninja Foodi.
Set dehydrator to 135 degrees F for 6 hours.
Once the time is complete takeout the mango slices and stores it into an airtight glass container.

Nutrition Facts

Servings: 4

Citrus Crisps

Cooking Time: 6 Hours
Yield: 2 Servings

2 grapefruit
2 blood oranges

Directions

The first step is to cut the fruits into very thin round slices, keep the peel intact.
Layer the round cut citrus on dehydrator racks.
Put the dehydrate rack inside the Ninja Foodi.
Turn on the Ninja Foodi and press dehydrates, and set the temperature to 135 degrees F and set time to 6 hours.
Once cooking time complete turn off the unit.
Open the Ninja Foodi and take out the chips.
Serve once cool down.

Nutrition Facts

Servings: 2
Amount per serving
Calories   127
% Daily Value*
Total Fat 0.4g   0%
Saturated Fat 0.1g 0%
Cholesterol 0mg   0%
Sodium 0mg   0%
Total Carbohydrate 32g 12%
Dietary Fiber 5.8g 21%
Total Sugars 26.1g
Protein 2.5g

Dehydrated Thyme in Ninja Food

Cooking Time: 6 Hours
Yield: 1 Cup

1-2 cups thyme

Directions

Leave the steam intake to leave.
Take a baking tray and layer it with aluminum foil.
Now place it inside Ninja Foodi.
Put thyme inside the baking tray.
Set temperature to 135 degrees F and sett timer to 6 hours.
Take out and scrape off the leaves and grind into a fine consistency.
Reserve in jars for further use.

Nutrition Facts

Servings: 2

Amount per serving
Calories 66
% Daily Value*
Total Fat 1.8g   2%
Saturated Fat 0.7g 3%
Cholesterol 0mg   0%
Sodium 13mg   1%
Total Carbohydrate 15.4g   6%
Dietary Fiber 8.9g 32%
Total Sugars 0.4g
Protein 2.2g

Dehydrated Rosemary in Ninja Foodi

Cooking Time: 6 Hours
Yield: ½ Cup

Ingredients

2 cups rosemary

Directions

Leave the steam intake to leave.
Take a baking tray and layer it with aluminum foil.
Now place rosemary inside the baking tray.
Put the tray in the Ninja Foodi grill.
Set temperature to 135 degrees and set the timer to 6 hours by turning on dehydrator.
Take out the tray and grind the rosemary.

Nutrition Facts

Servings: 2
Amount per serving
Calories   191
% Daily Value*
Total Fat 8.8g   11%
Saturated Fat 4.3g 21%
Cholesterol 0mg   0%
Sodium 29mg   1%
Total Carbohydrate 36.9g   13%
Dietary Fiber 24.5g 88%
Total Sugars 0g
Protein 2.8g

Teriyaki Beef Turkey

Cooking Time: 6 Hours
Yield: 2 Servings

Ingredients

1/2 cup of Teriyaki sauce
1/4 cup Liquid smoke
1 pound of beef, eye round thin cut

Directions

Cut the strip of beef into strips.
Take a zip lock bag and add strip along with teriyaki sauce and liquid smoke.
Let it seal and marinate for a few hours in the refrigerator.
After marinating time complete take out the strips.
Layer the strip on the dehydrating racks.
Place a rack inside Ninja Foodi and dehydrate for 6 hours at 135degreess F.
Once done take out and serve enjoy.

Nutrition Facts

Servings: 2

Amount per serving
Calories   469
% Daily Value*
Total Fat 14.1g   18%
Saturated Fat 5.3g 27%
Cholesterol 203mg   68%
Sodium 2219mg   96%
Total Carbohydrate 8.4g 3%
Dietary Fiber 0.1g 0%
Total Sugars 7.6g
Protein 72g

Dehydrating Sweet Potato in Ninja Foodi

Amount per serving
Calories   177
% Daily Value*
Total Fat 0.3g   0%
Saturated Fat 0.1g 0%
Cholesterol 0mg   0%
Sodium 14mg   1%
Total Carbohydrate 41.8g   15%
Dietary Fiber 6.2g 22%
Total Sugars 0.8g
Protein 2.3g

Cooking Time: 2 Hours
Yield: 2 Servings

Ingredients

2 large sweet potatoes, round cut

Directions

Peel the sweet potatoes and cut them in a very thin round shapes
Layer the round chips on to the dehydrating rack and place the rack inside the Ninja Foodi.
Set temperature to 195 degrees F.
Set time to 2 hours.
Take out and serve.

Nutrition Facts

Servings: 2

Dehydrated Potatoes Sticks

Nutrition Facts

Servings: 2
Amount per serving
Calories   255
% Daily Value*
Total Fat 0.4g   0%
Saturated Fat 0.1g 0%
Cholesterol 0mg   0%
Sodium 22mg   1%
Total Carbohydrate 58g 21%
Dietary Fiber 8.9g 32%
Total Sugars 4.2g
Protein 6.2g

Cooking Time: 2 Hours
Yield: 2 Servings

2 large potatoes, peeled and cut into thin slices like match-stick

Directions

Peel the potatoes and cut them in very thin shapes like a matchstick.
You can use an automatic round potato chip cutting machine to make the job done.
Layer the round chips on to the dehydrating rack and place the rack inside the Ninja Foodi.
Turn on the Ninja Foodi by pressing dehydrator option and set the temperature to 195 degrees F.
Set time to 2 hours.
Take out and serve.

Dehydrated Plum Tomatoes

Cooking Item: 9 Hours
Yield: 1/3 Cup

Ingredients

2 plum tomatoes
4 pinch of salt

Directions

Slice the plum tomatoes in half and then scrape out the seeds.
Now make a shallow slit into the skin.
Sprinkle some salt.
Drain any excess liquid.
Layer the plum tomatoes on the dehydrating racks and place rack inside the Ninja Foodi.
Set temperature to 135 to 140 F for 9 hours.
Once done, take out.

Nutrition Facts

Servings: 1
Amount per serving
Calories   57
% Daily Value*
Total Fat 0.5g   1%
Saturated Fat 0.1g 0%
Cholesterol 0mg   0%
Sodium 652mg   28%
Total Carbohydrate 12.6g   5%
Dietary Fiber 2.7g 10%
Total Sugars 9.8g
Protein 3g

Dehydrated Clementine's

Cooking Time: 6 Hours
Yield: 2 Servings

Ingredients

2 Clementine's, peeled
Salt and black pepper, to taste

Directions

The first step is to peel the Clementine's and slices then road very thinly.
 You can alas keep the peel intake if like the flavor   .
Sprinkle salt and black pepper on slices as per liking.
Layer the slices on dehydrating rack.
Put the dehydrate rack inside the Ninja Foodi
Turn on the Ninja Foodi and press dehydrate button, and set the temperature to 135 degrees F and set time to 6 hours.
Once cooking time complete turn off the Ninja Foodi.
Open the unit and take out the zesty and tangy Clementine jerky.
Serve once cool down.

Nutrition Facts

Servings: 2
Amount per serving
Calories   35
% Daily Value*
Total Fat 0.1g   0%
Saturated Fat 0g   0%
Cholesterol 0mg   0%
Sodium 1mg   0%
Total Carbohydrate 8.9g 3%
Dietary Fiber 1.3g 5%
Total Sugars 6.8g
Protein 0.6g

Dehydrated Apricots

Cooking Time: 6 Hours
Yield: 2 Servings

Ingredients

6 ripe apricots, not overly soften

Directions

Half the apricots by hands, and take out the seeds.
Slice the apricots in thin slices.
Layer the apricots on to the dehydrating rack.
Place the rack inside Ninja Foodi and close the hood.
Set the temperature to 140 degrees Fahrenheit and allow the apricots to dry for 15-18 hours.
Once the apricots are firm they are good to go.

Nutrition Facts

Servings: 2

Amount per serving
Calories   50
% Daily Value*
Total Fat 0.7g   1%
Saturated Fat 0g   0%
Cholesterol 0mg   0%
Sodium 1mg   0%
Total Carbohydrate 11.5g   4%
Dietary Fiber 2g   7%
Total Sugars 9.5g
Protein 1.4g

Beet Chips

Amount per serving
Calories 44
% Daily Value*
Total Fat 0.2g 0%
Saturated Fat 0g 0%
Cholesterol 0mg 0%
Sodium 77mg 3%
Total Carbohydrate 10g 4%
Dietary Fiber 2g 7%
Total Sugars 8g
Protein 1.7g

Cooking Time: 8 Hours
Yield: 2 Servings

Ingredients

2-3 beets, peeled and thinly sliced

Directions

Wash and cut the beetroots in thin slices abpti1/8 inches thin.
Layer the slices on to the dehydrating rack.
Place the rack inside Ninja Foodi and close the hood.
Set temperature to 135 degrees and set time to 8 hours.
Once done, serve.

Nutrition Facts

Servings: 2

Dehydrated Mandarin Orange

Cooking Time: 6 Hours
Yield: 2 Servings

Ingredients

2 Mandarin Oranges, peeled

Directions

The first step is to peel the mandarin oranges.
Slice in to round thin slices. .
Layer the slices on dehydrating rack.
Put the dehydrate rack inside the Ninja Foodi.
Turn on the Ninja Foodi and press the dehydrate and set the temperature to 135 degrees F and set time to 5 hours.
Afterward, open the unit and take out dehydrated pieces
Serve once cool.

Nutrition Facts

Servings: 2
Amount per serving
Calories   92
% Daily Value*
Total Fat 0.1g   0%
Saturated Fat 0g   0%
Cholesterol 0mg   0%
Sodium 12mg   1%
Total Carbohydrate 23.8g   9%
Dietary Fiber 1.7g 6%
Total Sugars 22.1g
Protein 1.5g

Chapter No 4:20 Baked Recipes by Ninja Foodi Grill

Baked Skillet Cookies in Ninja Foodi

Cooking Time: 23 Minutes
Yield: 6 Servings

Ingredients

1 cup -1/4 cup of tablespoons all-purpose flour
1/3 teaspoon baking soda
1/4 teaspoon kosher salt
1 stick unsalted butter, softened, plus more for greasing
8 tablespoons granulated sugar
4 tablespoons packed brown sugar
1 teaspoon vanilla extract
1 large egg
1-1/2 cup semi-sweet chocolate chips
1 cup chopped walnuts, chopped

Directions

Close the crisping lid of the Ninja Foodi and select bake /roast.
Set the time to 5 minutes at 325 degrees for preheating.
Select start.
Meanwhile in a mixing bowl beat together flour, baking soda, salt.
In a separate bowl beat together sugar, butter, vanilla until creamy.
Add eggs and beat until smooth.
Now combine ingredients of both the bowls.
Make sure not to over
In the end, fold in the chocolate chip and walnuts
Mix and generously grease the bottom of the Ninja Foodi and add cookie dough onto the pan.
Evenly disturbed it.
Once the preheating is done, open the unit.
Close crisping lid. Select BAKE/ROAST, set temperature to 325°F, for 23 minutes.
Select START/STOP to begin.
When cooking is complete, allow the cookie to cool for 10 minutes.
Then serve warm.

Nutrition Facts

Servings: 6
Amount per serving
Calories   504
% Daily Value*
Total Fat 35.3g   45%
Saturated Fat 12.7g 64%
Cholesterol 71mg   24%
Sodium 383mg   17%
Total Carbohydrate 43.7g   16%
Dietary Fiber 2.5g   9%
Total Sugars 33.1g

Bake Potatoes in Ninja Foodi Grill

Cooking Time: 50 Minutes
Yield: 2 Servings

Ingredients

2 large russet potatoes, skin on
2 tablespoons of grapeseed oil
Sea salt, to taste

Topping Ingredients

1/4 cup bacon
1/2 cup mild cheddar cheese
1/4 cup of butter
Salt and black pepper
1/2 cup sour cream

Directions

Rub the potatoes with grape seed oil and sprinkle salt on top.
Place the potatoes inside Ninja Foodi and close lid.
Select bake/ roast.
Cook for 45 minutes.
Turn it once after 20 minutes.
Once done take out and shut the Foodi off.
Now cut the potato lengthwise with a knife.
Open up the cavity of the potatoes and start to top it with the entire listed topping ingredient.
Now put potatoes in Ninja Foodi for the cheese to melt.
Select broil and start cooking for a few minutes.
Once the cheese melts, takeout and serves.

Nutrition Facts

Servings: 2
Amount per serving
Calories   818
% Daily Value*
Total Fat 59g   76%
Saturated Fat 29.2g   146%
Cholesterol 117mg   39%
Sodium 520mg   23%
Total Carbohydrate 60.9g   22%
Dietary Fiber 8.9g 32%
Total Sugars 4.5g
Protein 15.5g

Ninja Foodi Baked Gluten-Free Oatmeal

Cooking Time: 30 Minutes
Yield: 4 Serving

Ingredients

4 Cups gluten-free oats
1/2 teaspoon Baking Powder
Salt, pinch
3-4 small Eggs
1-2 cups coconut milk
1 Cup applesauce

Directions

Combine and whisk together all the listed ingredients in the large mixing bowl.
Spray the bottom of the Ninja Foodi with a cooking spray like canola oil spray.
Evenly spread the oatmeal mixture in the Ninja Foodi.
Use the "Bake" function and set a timer for 30 minutes at 325 degrees F.
Once done, serve with additional milk.

Nutrition Facts

Servings: 4
Amount per serving
Calories   515
% Daily Value*
Total Fat 22.4g   29%
Saturated Fat 14.5g   72%
Cholesterol 103mg   34%
Sodium 93mg   4%
Total Carbohydrate 66.1g   24%
Dietary Fiber 10.3g 37%
Total Sugars 9.2g
Protein 15.7g

Baked Fish in Ninja Foodi

Cooking Time: 15 Minutes
Yield: 1 Serving

Ingredients

1 fish fillet, skin on
1/2 Cilantro
1/2 onions
4 garlic cloves
2 tablespoons of Butter
Old bay seasoning to taste
Salt and black pepper, to taste
1 lemon, sliced

Directions

Preheat Ninja Foodi for 5 minutes by pressing bake/roast.
Make few cuts on the outer skin of the fish, so the seasoning gets inside.
Fill the inner cavity of fish with butter. Then season it salt, black paper, and old bay seasoning.
Add garlic in the inner pocket of the fish.
Now rub the butter on to the skin and season the skin with old bay seasoning, salt, and black pepper.
Put fish on a piece of aluminum foil and top it with pieces of lemon.
Make a packet of aluminum foil.
Put trivet inside Ninja Foodi.
Place aluminum foil pocket on top of the trivet.
Bake it at 100 degrees F for 20minutes.
Once done shut down the unit and uncover the fish.
Bake for 5 more minutes.
Serve hot.

Nutrition Facts

Servings: 1
Amount per serving
Calories   455
% Daily Value*
Total Fat 34.4g   44%
Saturated Fat 17.2g   86%
Cholesterol 92mg 31%
Sodium 733mg   32%
Total Carbohydrate 24.7g   9%
Dietary Fiber 2g   7%
Total Sugars 2.5g
Protein 15g

Fish and Grits

Cooking Time: 30 Minutes
Yield: 2 Serving

Ingredients

3 cups chicken broth
1 cup heavy cream
1 cup grits
Salt and black pepper, to taste
4 tablespoons of butter
2 tilapia fish fillets, 4 ounces each
1 teaspoon of old bay seasoning
2 tablespoons of avocado oil

Directions

Add broth, heavy cream, grits, salt, and black pepper, butter in a Ninja Foodi.
Whisk ingredients together.
Close the Ninja Foodi with a pressure cooker cover.
Seal it properly.
Cook on high for 10 minutes.
Meanwhile, coat the fish fillet with avocado oil spray.
Season it with old bay seasoning.
Once cooking is done, release steam and open the Ninja Foodi.
The texture will be nice and creamy.
Put a piece of foil on top of the mixture inside Ninja Foodi.
Now put the fillet on top of the foil.
Bake it at100 for20minutes.
Once done, serve.

Nutrition Facts

Servings: 2
Amount per serving
Calories   796
% Daily Value*
Total Fat 61.8g   79%
Saturated Fat 31.5g   157%
Cholesterol 168mg   56%
Sodium 2305mg   100%
Total Carbohydrate 38.6g   14%
Dietary Fiber 3.7g   13%
Total Sugars 3.7g
Protein 22.1g

Ninja Foodi Baked Pumpkin Oatmeal

Cooking Time: 30 Minutes
Yield: 4 Servings

Ingredients

4 Cups Old Fashioned Oat
1/2 Cup Brown Sugar
1/2 teaspoon Baking Powder
Salt, pinch
2 teaspoons of Cinnamon
4 teaspoons of Pumpkin Pie Spice
1 teaspoon of Nutmeg
3-4 small Eggs
1-2 Cups Milk
1 Cup Pumpkin Puree

Directions

Combine and whisk together all the listed ingredients in the large mixing bowl.
Spray the inner bottom of the unit with cooking spray such as grape seed oil. Evenly spread the oatmeal mixture inside the coated Ninja Foodi.
Use the "Bake" function and set a timer for 30 minutes at 325 degrees F.
Once done, serve with milk.

Nutrition Facts

Servings: 4
Amount per serving
Calories   796
% Daily Value*
Total Fat 14.9g   19%
Saturated Fat 4g   20%
Cholesterol 108mg   36%
Sodium 116mg   5%
Total Carbohydrate 136g   49%
Dietary Fiber 18.4g 66%
Total Sugars 27.1g
Protein 26.4g

Baked Western Omelets

Cooking Time: 35 Minutes
Yield: 10 Servings

Ingredients

10 eggs
1/3 cup milk
Salt and pepper, to taste
1-1/2 cup shredded cheddar cheese
1-1/2 cup cooked ham, diced
1/2 cup red bell pepper, diced
1/34 cup green bell pepper, diced

Directions

Preheat the Ninja Foodi grill by closing the crisping lid and selecting the bake/roast button.
Set the timer to 5 minutes at 315 degrees F.
Meanwhile, take a mixing bowl and whisk together eggs, milk, salt, and pepper.
Then add cheese, ham, red bell pepper, and green bell pepper.
Mix all the ingredients.
Generously grease the bottom of the Ninja Foodi baking pan with oil spray.
Pour egg mixture into the pan.
Place the rack inside Ninja Foodi and put the pan on top.
Lock the Ninja Foodi and select bake/roast.
Set temperate to 315 degrees F for 35 minutes.
Select start.
Once the omelet is ready, serve and enjoy.

Nutrition Facts

Servings: 10
Amount per serving
Calories   137
% Daily Value*
Total Fat 9.5g   12%
Saturated Fat 4.2g 21%
Cholesterol 184mg   61%
Sodium 312mg   14%
Total Carbohydrate 1.9g 1%
Dietary Fiber 0.3g   1%
Total Sugars 1.1g
Protein 10.9g

Cheesy Egg Bake

Cooking Time: 30 Minutes
Yield: 3 Servings

Ingredients

6 slices bacon, chopped
6 eggs
1/3 cup of coconut milk
1/2 cup shredded cheddar cheese
Salt and black pepper, to taste
2 green onion, chopped

Directions

Preheat the Ninja Foodi grill by closing the crisping lid and selecting the bake/roast button.
Set a timer to 5 minutes at 315 degrees F.
Meanwhile, take a mixing bowl and whisk together all the listed ingredients
Generously grease the bottom of the Ninja Foodi baking pan with oil spray.
Pour the egg mixture into the pan and adjust the pan on top of the rack.
Put the rack inside Ninja Foodi.
Close the Ninja Foodi and select back/roast.
Set temperature to 300 degrees F, for 30 minutes.
Once done, serve.

Nutrition Facts

Servings: 3
Amount per serving
Calories   472
% Daily Value*
Total Fat 37.3g   48%
Saturated Fat 17.6g   88%
Cholesterol 389mg   130%
Sodium 1124mg   49%
Total Carbohydrate 3.7g 1%
Dietary Fiber 0.9g 3%
Total Sugars 1.9g
Protein 30.6g

Mushroom and Egg Omelets

Cooking Time: 35 Minutes
Yield: 5 Servings

Ingredients

10 eggs
1/3 cup milk
Salt and pepper, to taste
1-1/2 cup shredded cheddar cheese
1-1/2 cup mushrooms
1/2 cup black olives
1/4 cup fresh chives, diced

Directions

Preheat the Ninja Foodi grill by closing the crisping lid and selecting the bake/roast button.
Set a timer to 10 minutes at 315 degrees F.
Meanwhile, take a large bowl and whisk together eggs, milk, salt, and black pepper.
Then add cheese, mushroom, and back olive along with chives.
Mix all the ingredients.
Generously grease the bottom of the Ninja Foodi baking pan with avocado oil spray.
Pour egg mixture into the pan.
Place a rack inside Ninja Foodi and put the pan on top.
Lock the Ninja Foodi and select bake/roast.
Set temperate to 315 degrees F for 35 minutes.
Select start.
Once done, serve and enjoy.

Nutrition Facts

Servings: 5
Amount per serving
Calories   244
% Daily Value*
Total Fat 18.1g   23%
Saturated Fat 7.9g 39%
Cholesterol 352mg   117%
Sodium 389mg   17%
Total Carbohydrate 3.2g 1%
Dietary Fiber 0.6g 2%
Total Sugars 1.8g
Protein 17.9g

Hash Brown

Cooking Time: 40 Minutes
Yield: 8 Servings

Ingredients

8 eggs
46 ounces of hash brown, frozen
1/2 cup milk
1 large onion
4 tablespoons of olive oil
1.26 pound Ham
1 cup cheddar cheese

Directions

Preheat the Ninja Foodi grill by turning on the bake /roast button for 10 minutes at 315 minutes.
In a medium bowl mix together hash browns, milk onions, olive oil, ham, and cheddar cheese.
Whisk eggs in a separate bowl and combine ingredients of both the bowls. Grease a baking pan of Foodi gill with oil spray and pour a mixture of egg in it. Place a rack inside the Ninja Foodi and then put the pan on top of the rack. Lock the lid and then select bake/roast. Set temperature to 315 and set the timer to 40 minutes.
Select the start and then wait for the time to complete it.
Once done, take out and serve.

Nutrition Facts

Servings: 8
Amount per serving
Calories   743
% Daily Value*
Total Fat 42.9g   55%
Saturated Fat 10.7g   54%
Cholesterol 220mg   73%
Sodium 1646mg   72%
Total Carbohydrate 63g 23%
Dietary Fiber 6.6g 23%
Total Sugars 4.3g
Protein

Baked Salmon in Ninja Foodi Grill

Cooking Time: 30 Minutes
Yield: 2 Servings

Ingredients

6 ounces salmon fillets, skin, and bones removed
1 teaspoon olive oil
Kosher salt, to taste
Black pepper, to taste

Directions

Rinse and pat dry salmon fillets.
Grease the salmon fillet from both sides with oil
Season both sides with salt and black pepper.
Preheat Ninja Foodi for 5 minutes by pressing bake/roast.
Put trivet inside Ninja Foodi.
Place fish on top of aluminum foil and close it in the shape of the pocket.
Place aluminum foil pocket on top of the trivet.
Put salmon on top of aluminum foil.
Bake it at 100 for 15-25 minutes.
Once done shut down the unit and uncover the fish.
Roast for 5 more minutes.

Nutrition Facts

Servings: 2
Amount per serving
Calories   133
% Daily Value*
Total Fat 7.6g   10%
Saturated Fat 1.1g 5%
Cholesterol 38mg 13%
Sodium 115mg   5%
Total Carbohydrate 0g   0%
Dietary Fiber 0g   0%
Total Sugars 0g
Protein 16.5g

Pound Cake in Ninja Foodi

Cooking Time: 35 Minutes
Yield: 3 Servings

Ingredients

2 sticks butter
1 cup of Sugar
4 large eggs room temp
1 tbsp vanilla extract
1/2 pounds flour
1 orange zest only
1 tbsp butter for greasing pan
3 tablespoons powdered sugar

Directions

Take a large bowl and use a stand mixer to mix butter and sugar.
Once the mixture is fluffy add eggs, one at a time.
Mix to incorporate the ingredients well. Repeat until all eggs are mixed.
Now add vanilla, flour and start stand mixer to mix the ingredients in fine consistency.
Then add zest and Stir well.
Butter a 6- 7 inch of ring mold pan.
Pour two cups of water inside the Ninja Foodi.
Put the rack inside at a low position.
Put the cake pan on top of the rack.
Cover the cake top with aluminum cover.
Set pressure on high for 25 minutes.
When the time completes, allow to natural release for 20 minutes*.
Take out the cake and place it on a baking rack for cooling.
Return the cake to the Ninja food and select bake/roast.
Cook for 10 minutes at 400 degrees F.
Once golden from the top take out and save.

Nutrition Facts

Servings: 3
Amount per serving
Calories   1340
% Daily Value*
Total Fat 83.5g   107%
Saturated Fat 50.6g   253%
Cholesterol 450mg   150%
Sodium 639mg   28%
Total Carbohydrate 133.4g   49%
Dietary Fiber 2g   7%
Total Sugars 76.1g
Protein 17g

4 Ingredients Nutella Cake

Cooking Time: 25 Minutes
Yields: 2 Servings

Ingredients

1 cup of Sugar-free Nut-light
2 eggs, whisked
1/2 cup almond flour
6 raspberries, chopped

Directions

Take a bowl and whisk eggs in it.
Then add nut light and whisk well for a fine combination.
Next, add flour to the mixture and finely incorporate it
Oil grease egg bites mold.
Divide the mixture between molds.
Top each meld with raspberries.
Now pour 2 cups water in Ninja Foodi.
Place rack at the lower position of the Ninja Foodi.
Put the egg mold on top of the rack.
Set pressure on high for 20 minutes.
When the time completes, allow to natural release for 20 minutes*.
Take out the cake and place it on a baking rack for cooling.
Return the cake t the Ninja Foodi and select bake/roast.
Cook for 5 minutes at 400 degrees F.
Once done, serve.

Nutrition Facts

Servings: 2
Amount per serving
Calories   533
% Daily Value*
Total Fat 48.2g   62%
Saturated Fat 9.6g 48%
Cholesterol 164mg   55%
Sodium 1102mg   48%
Total Carbohydrate 8.7g 3%
Dietary Fiber 4.5g   16%
Total Sugars 3.1g
Protein 7.7g

Ninja Foodi Pumpkin Bread

Cooking Time: 40 Minutes
Yield: 4 Servings

Ingredients

1/3 cup pumpkin puree (canned)
3 eggs
1/2 cup of vegetable oil
1/4 cup water
1 cup of sugar
1-1/2 cup gluten-free all-purpose flour
3/4 teaspoons baking soda
Salt, pinch
1/3 teaspoon ground cinnamon
1/3 teaspoon of nutmeg
1 teaspoon pumpkin pie spice
Powdered sugar, for sprinkling

Directions

In a mixing bowl combine eggs, oil, water, and pumpkin.
Use a stand mixer to mix well
Combine remaining ingredients in a separate noel
Mix ingredients of both the bowls
Once the dough is formed pour it into a loaf pan.
Place the pan on the wire rack.
Put the rack inside Ninja Foodi.
Shut the unit and turn on the bake function.
Set temperate to 325 degrees F for 40 minutes.
Once done, remove it from the Ninja Foodi and let it get cool.
Sprinkle with powdered sugar then serve.

Nutrition Facts

Servings: 4
Amount per serving
Calories   651
% Daily Value*
Total Fat 31.5g   40%
Saturated Fat 3.1g 16%
Cholesterol 123mg   41%
Sodium 322mg   14%
Total Carbohydrate 87.4g   32%
Dietary Fiber 5.3g 19%
Total Sugars 53g
Protein 8.9g

Monkey Bread

Cooking Time: 40 Minutes
Yield: 4 Servings

Ingredients

1 cup bananas puree
2 eggs
1/2 cup of butter
1/2 cup of sugar
2 cups gluten-free flour
1/3 teaspoon of baking soda
1 1/2 teaspoons ground cinnamon
1/4 cup pecans chopped and lightly toasted

Directions

Take a large mixing bowl and whisk eggs in it.
Then add sugar, banana puree, and butter.
Use a hand mixer to beat the ingredients to a fine consistency.
Then add flour, baking soda, cinnamon, and pecan.
Mix into a fine smooth consistency.
Oil grease a loaf pan and pours the mixture into the pan.
Place the pan on the wire rack.
Put the rack inside Ninja Foodi.
Shut the unit and turn on the bake function.
Set temperate to 335 degrees F for 35-40 minutes.
Once done, remove it from the Ninja Foodi, and let it get cool by placing it on a cooling rack.
Once cool, slice and serve.

Nutrition Facts

Servings: 4
Amount per serving
Calories   614
% Daily Value*
Total Fat 26.4g   34%
Saturated Fat 15.7g   79%
Cholesterol 143mg   48%
Sodium 1031mg   45%
Total Carbohydrate 92.3g   34%
Dietary Fiber 8.6g 31%
Total Sugars 40.9g
Protein 7.3g

Walnuts and Raspberries Cake

Cooking Time: 35 Minutes
Yield: 4 Servings

Ingredients

8 tablespoons of butter
1/3 teaspoon of cinnamon
1 cup walnuts, crushed
1 cup raspberries
1/3 cup of plain milk
1/3 cup sugar
2 cups of almond flour
4 eggs, whisked
1/4 teaspoon of baking soda

Directions

Mix butter, sugar, and cinnamon in a large mixing bowl.
Once fluffy, add walnuts, baking soda, raspberries, milk, and almond flour.
Then add the whisked eggs, mix the ingredients into a smooth batter.
Spoon the mixture to an oil greased small loaf pan.
Place the pan on the wire rack.
Put the rack inside Ninja Foodi.
Shut the unit and turn on the bake function.
Set temperate to 325 degrees F for 35 minutes.
Once done, serve.

Nutrition Facts

Servings: 4
Amount per serving
Calories   635
% Daily Value*
Total Fat 53.4g   68%
Saturated Fat 17.9g   90%
Cholesterol 227mg   76%
Sodium 320mg   14%
Total Carbohydrate 27.9g   10%
Dietary Fiber 5.7g   20%
Total Sugars 19.7g
Protein 17.4g

Ninja Foodi Lemon Cream Cheese Dump Cake

Cooking Time: 30 Minutes
Yield: 4 Servings

Ingredients

16 ounces lemon pie filling
16 ounces yellow cake mix
6 ounces cream cheese cut into small pieces
1/2 cup butter cut into thin slices, additional 2 tbsp

Directions

Oil greases the cooking pot with oil spray.
Layer the lemon pie fling on the bottom of the cooking pot.
Top it with half of the cake mix.
Put some cream cheese on top and cover it with the remaining cake mix.
In the end, top it with butter and cover all areas of cake with butter.
Select bake
Set temperature to 350 degrees for 30 minutes
Start the unit
After 30 minutes test the cake with a toothpick that it comes out clean
Scoop out the dump cake on to serving plates and enjoy

Nutrition Facts

Servings: 4
Amount per serving
Calories   995
% Daily Value*
Total Fat 51.7g   66%
Saturated Fat 25.9g   129%
Cholesterol 129mg   43%
Sodium 1314mg   57%
Total Carbohydrate 126.6g   46%
Dietary Fiber 1.3g 4%
Total Sugars 81.1g
Protein 8.4g

Ninja Foodi Apple Dump Cake

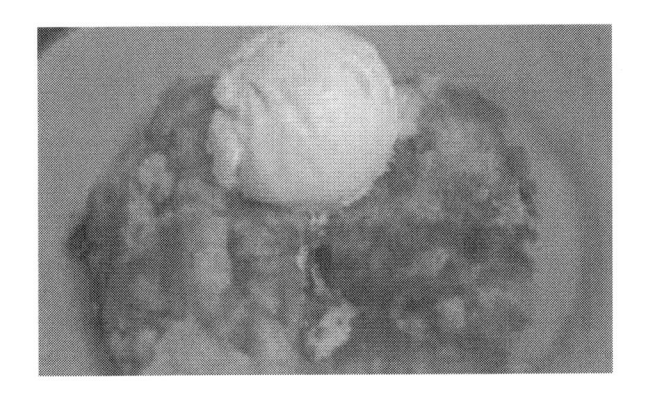

Cooking Time: 25 Minutes
Yield: 4 Servings

Ingredients

22 ounces of apple pie filling
15 ounces of yellow cake mix
6 ounces cream cheese cut into small pieces
1/3 cup butter cut into thin slices

Directions

Oil greases a tin pan with oil spray.
Spread apple pie filling in the bottom of a tin pan.
Top it with 3/4 of the dry cake mix.
Then add the cream cheese layer on top.
Pour the remaining cake mix on top evenly.
Top it with butter in a single layer.
Cover all areas of cake.
Place the tin into the cooking pot of Ninja Foodi.
Close the crisping lid.
Select BAKE/ROAST and set the timer to 25miutes at 350 degrees F.
Once the toothpick comes out clean the cake is ready.
Serve and enjoy.

Nutrition Facts

Servings: 4
Amount per serving
Calories   899
% Daily Value*
Total Fat 42.7g   55%
Saturated Fat 20.9g   105%
Cholesterol 90mg   30%
Sodium 1007mg   44%
Total Carbohydrate 124.9g   45%
Dietary Fiber 2.7g   10%
Total Sugars 67.7g
Protein 8.2g

Chocolate Chip Cookie Cake

Nutrition Facts

Servings: 4
Amount per serving
Calories   240
% Daily Value*
Total Fat 12g   15%
Saturated Fat 4g   20%
Cholesterol 20mg   7%
Sodium 210mg   9%
Total Carbohydrate 34g 12%
Dietary Fiber 2g   7%
Total Sugars 20g
Protein 2g

Cooking Time: 15 Minutes
Yield: 4 Servings

Ingredients

8 scoops chocolate chip cookie dough
Non-stick butter spray to coat the pan

Directions

Grease the cake pan with oil spray.
Scoop the cookie dough into the cake pan by press firmly.
Set the pan on the trivet and put trivet on the inner bottom of Ninja Foodi.
Set the Ninja Foodi on 325 on Bake for 15 minutes.
Once cookies are firm, take out and serve

Baked Jerk Chicken

Cooking Time: 30 Minutes
Yield: 4 Servings

Ingredients

1 teaspoon ground allspice
2 teaspoons ground cinnamon
2 teaspoons ground thyme
2 teaspoons ground nutmeg
1 small ginger - peeled
4 clove garlic - peeled
4 tablespoons of canola oil
4 sprigs green onion
2 lime, juiced
2 tablespoons of vinegar
10 chicken pieces
Salt, to taste

Directions

Put all the ingredients except chicken in the blender and pulse into a fine paste. Rub the chicken with the blended marinate.
Refrigerate the chicken for 4 hours.
Next, put the cook and a crisp basket inside the unit of Ninja Foodi.
Place marinated chicken in the basket Put the pressure lid on top and select pressure.
Set it to high for 20 minutes.
Afterward, turn on bake and then cook it for 10 minutes at 400 degrees F.

Nutrition Facts

Servings: 4
Amount per serving
Calories   849
% Daily Value*
Total Fat 41.7g   53%
Saturated Fat 8.8g 44%
Cholesterol 325mg   108%
Sodium 358mg   16%
Total Carbohydrate 7.8g 3%
Dietary Fiber 2.5g 9%
Total Sugars 1.3g
Protein 106.5g

Chapter No 5:20 Roasted Recipes by Ninja Foodi Grill

Herbed Chicken

Cooking Time: 32 Minutes
Yield: 8 Servings

Ingredients

4 pounds of whole uncooked chicken
1 Cup lemon juice
1/4 cup honey
Salt, to taste
1/4 cup hot water
1 tablespoon whole black peppercorns
6 sprigs fresh thyme
8 cloves garlic, peeled, smashed
2 tablespoon canola oil

Directions

Remove any giblets inside the cavity of the chicken.
Take a small bowl and mix lemon juice, hot water, salt, and honey.
Pour it to cook and crisp basket.
Rub chicken with thyme, peppercorn, and garlic.
Place chicken in cook and crisp basket.
Place the basket inside the Ninja Foodi pot.
Lock the pot with pressure lid.
Set to high for 22 minutes.
Once done release pressure naturally for 10 minutes.
Carefully remove the lid from the top.
Brush chicken with canola oil and season it with salt and pepper.
Close crisping lid.
Select roast and set the temperature to 400°F, and set time to 10 minutes.
Once done, serve.

Nutrition Facts

Servings: 8
Amount per serving
Calories   565
% Daily Value*
Total Fat 40.3g   52%
Saturated Fat 10.7g   53%
Cholesterol 233mg   78%
Sodium 230mg   10%
Total Carbohydrate 11.4g   4%
Dietary Fiber 0.7g   2%
Total Sugars 9.4g
Protein 39.1g

Lemon Chicken

Cooking Time: 30 Minutes
Yield: 8 Servings

Ingredients

4 pounds of chicken, whole
1/2 cup of Lemon juice
1/3 cup of Honey
Salt, to taste
Black pepper, to taste
1/4 cup hot water

Directions

Take a bowl and mix lemon juice, honey, salt, black paper, and water.
Pour the liquid in the roasting basket.
Put the chicken inside the roasting basket
Put pressure lid on.
Pressure cook on high for 22 minutes.
Once done, take off the pressure lid, by releasing pressure naturally of 15 minutes.
Sprinkle salt and black pepper on top of the chicken and then close the hood of Ninja Foodi.
Press roast and cook for 10 minutes at 400 degrees f.
Serve and enjoy.

Nutrition Facts

Servings: 8
Amount per serving
Calories   389
% Daily Value*
Total Fat 7g 9%
Saturated Fat 2.1g 10%
Cholesterol 175mg   58%
Sodium 166mg   7%
Total Carbohydrate 12g 4%
Dietary Fiber 0.1g 0%
Total Sugars 11.9g
 Protein 65.9g

Beef Chuck Roast with Root Vegetables

Cooking Time: 45 Minutes
Yield: 4 Servings

Ingredients

2 pounds of beef chuck roast
14 ounce can beef broth
5 ounces of water
Salt and black pepper, to taste
1 teaspoon of garlic powder
1 onion, chopped
1 turnip, peeled and chopped
2 carrots, peeled and chopped

Directions

Pour the liquids, water, and broth, in the roasting basket.
Rub the roast with salt, black pepper, and garlic powder.
Place roast in the basket and put it inside the unit.
Put pressure lid on.
Pressure cook on high for 15 minutes.
Meanwhile cut the roots vegetables.
Once the time complete, release the pressure.
Take off the lid and remove the beef chunk onto the cooling rack.
Add chopped vegetables inside the basket and bake/ roast the vegetables for 25 minutes at 400 degrease.
Once time complete release the pressure and open the lid.
Put back the roast inside the basket.
Turn on sear and cook on high for a few minutes.
Once done, serve.
Enjoy.

Nutrition Facts

Servings: 4
Amount per serving
Calories   865
% Daily Value*
Total Fat 63.4g   81%
Saturated Fat 25.2g   126%
Cholesterol 234mg   78%
Sodium 512mg   22%
Total Carbohydrate 8.1g 3%
Dietary Fiber 2g   7%
Total Sugars 4g
Protein 61.4g

Ninja Foodi Pressure Cooker Pot Roast Recipe

Cooking Time: 1 Hour 40 Minutes
Yield: 8 Servings

Ingredients

4 pounds of Beef Bottom Round Roast
2 tablespoons of Ranch Seasoning Mix
1/3 cup warm water
2 teaspoons of Beef Bouillon cubes
10 tablespoons of Salted Butter
8 Greek pepperoncini Peppers

Directions

Open the Ninja Foodi and place roast inside it.
Mix bouillon cubes in warm water.
Rub the roast with the spice mixture and pour the bouillon broth on top.
Place a stick of butter and the peppers on top.
Twist & lock the pressure cooker lid.
Turn the vent to seal.
Pressure cooks it for 1 hour.
Allow pressure release normally for 25 minutes.
Once time complete now press roast and cook for 40 minutes at 400 degrees F.
Serve and enjoy

Nutrition Facts

Servings: 8
Amount per serving
Calories   531
% Daily Value*
Total Fat 29.1g   37%
Saturated Fat 14.3g   71%
Cholesterol 238mg   79%
Sodium 326mg   14%
Total Carbohydrate 0g   0%
Dietary Fiber 0g   0%
Total Sugars 0g
Protein 63.1g

Pork Roast

Cooking Time: 45 Minutes
Yield: 6 Servings

Ingredients

3 pounds Top Round Roast, pork

Ingredients

2 teaspoons sea salt
2 teaspoons pepper, crushed
2-1/2 teaspoon onion powders
2-1/2 teaspoon garlic powders

Directions

Combine all the seasoning in a bowl and apply it to the roast.
Preheat the Ninja Foodi grill by pressing the start and set temperate to 5 minutes.
Once preheating is done, open the unit and place the rack in the low position.
Place roast on rack and pressure cook for 20 minutes at high.
Once time complete, release pressure Now press roast and cook for 25 minutes at 400 degrees F.
Serve and enjoy.

Nutrition Facts

Servings: 6
Amount per serving
Calories   495
% Daily Value*
Total Fat 20.1g   26%
Saturated Fat 7g   35%
Cholesterol 191mg   64%
Sodium 763mg   33%
Total Carbohydrate 1.7g 1%
Dietary Fiber 0.2g 1%
Total Sugars 0.6g
Protein 72.2g

BBQ Ribs

Cooking Time: 45 Minutes
Yield: 4 Servings

Ingredients

1 rack of baby back ribs, 2 pounds
2 tablespoons barbecue meat rub
4 ounces of barbecue sauce, Keto-friendly
Canola oil spray

Directions

First coat the ribs with oil spray from all the sides.
Rub the baby back rib with the BBQ meat rub.
Preheat the Ninja Foodi grill by pressing the start and setting the temperature to 5 minutes.
Once done with preheating open then unit and place rack inside it.
Place the baby back ribs on top of the rack and pressure cook for 20 minutes at high.
Release pressure naturally.
Once done, open the lid of the Ninja Foodi and baste the ribs all over with the BBQ sauce.
Now, press roast and set the timer to 25 minutes at 400 degrees F.
Once done, serve.

Nutrition Facts

Servings: 4
Amount per serving
Calories   334
% Daily Value*
Total Fat 18.7g   24%
Saturated Fat 6.5g   33%
Cholesterol 0mg   0%
Sodium 812mg   35%
Total Carbohydrate 13.3g   5%
Dietary Fiber 0.2g   1%
Total Sugars 7.4g
Protein 0g

Ninja Foodi Rosemary Roast and Potatoes

Cooking Time: 45 Minutes
Yield: 4 Servings

Ingredients

4 gold potatoes, quartered
1/4 cup white onion, sliced
4 tablespoons of butter
1/3 cup white cooking wine
1/4 lemon, sliced
2 pounds beef chuck roast
2 tablespoons p dried rosemary
2 tablespoons of garlic minced
Salt and black pepper, to taste

Directions

Place potatoes in diet he Ninja Foodi and top it with onions.
Add butter and place roast on top.
Sprinkle rosemary, salt pepper, and garlic.
Pour cooing wine all over.
Close the lid and cook on low for an hour.
Begin by placing the potatoes on the bottom of the Ninja Foodi.
Top with the sliced onion.
Slice up the 2 tablespoons butter and place around the potatoes and onion.
Place the roast on top of it.
Sprinkle with rosemary, garlic, salt, and pepper.
Pour wine over the dish.
Top with sliced lemon.
Cover and pressure cook at high for 25 minutes
Once done, open the lid.
Put remaining butter on top.
Now, bake/roast for 30 minutes at 400 degrees F.
Serve.

Nutrition Facts

Servings: 4
Amount per serving
Calories   1207
% Daily Value*
Total Fat 76g   97%
Saturated Fat 32.8g   164%
Cholesterol 265mg   88%
Sodium 287mg   12%
Total Carbohydrate 63.2g   23%
Dietary Fiber 5.8g 21%
Total Sugars 3.1g
Protein 65.1g

Ninja Foodi Roast Chicken

Cooking Time: 45 Minutes
Yield: 6-8 Servings

Ingredients

4 pounds whole chicken
5 cloves garlic, peeled and crushed
3/4 cup hot water
1 cup dry rub, personal choice
2 tablespoons butter, melted

Directions

Clean, wash and pat dry the chicken.
Pour water in Ninja Foodi and then add garlic.
Sprinkle chicken with a dry rub and coat all over.
Set Cook & Crisp Basket inside the unit
Place chicken in basket breast side up.
Seal the unit by assembling the pressure lid.
Select PRESSURE and set to high for 20 minutes.
When time completes, allow to natural release for 12 minutes.
Carefully remove the lid and brush the chicken with melted butter.
Close the hood and press the Roast/Bake.
Adjust temperate to 400° Fahrenheit for 25 minutes.
Once the internal temperature reaches 165 degrees Fahrenheit it done, serve.

Nutrition Facts

Servings: 8
Amount per serving
Calories   371
% Daily Value*
Total Fat 9.8g   13%
Saturated Fat 3.8g 19%
Cholesterol 182mg   61%
Sodium 164mg   7%
Total Carbohydrate 0.6g 0%
Dietary Fiber 0g   0%
Total Sugars 0g
Protein 65.9g

Ninja Foodi Prime Rib

Cooking Time: 1 Hour 10 Minutes
Yield: 8 Servings

Ingredients

4 pounds of the rib roast
4 tablespoons of butter
Garlic salt, to taste
Black pepper, to taste

Directions

Season the meat with a generous amount of garlic salt, and black pepper.
Put the meat on an aluminum foiled covered trivet.
Rub butter on both sides.
Place butter on top as well.
Place the trivet inside Ninja Foodi.
First, turn on air crisp and cook for 10 minutes at 400 degrees F.
Once top gets nicely crisp, now add some more butter on top
Now press roast for 1 hour at 350 degrees F.
Once done, serve.

Nutrition Facts

Servings: 8
Amount per serving
Calories   536
% Daily Value*
Total Fat 28.7g   37%
Saturated Fat 11.7g   58%
Cholesterol 204mg   68%
Sodium 154mg   7%
Total Carbohydrate 0g   0%
Dietary Fiber 0g   0%
Total Sugars 0g
Protein 65.4g

Ninja Foodi Pot Roast

Cooking Time: 85-90 Minutes
Yield: 6 Servings

Ingredients

4 tablespoon of vegetable oil
3 pounds of chuck roast
Salt, to taste
2 cups beef broth
1/2 tsp sage
1/2 tsp black pepper
1/2 teaspoon crushed red pepper
1 pound baby carrots
1/2 pound mushrooms

Directions

Select sear/sauté on the Ninja Foodi and start the unit.
Allow preheating for 5 minutes.
Add vegetable oil to the Ninja Foodi pot.
Pat dry the beef roast.
Add beef to preheat the pot.
Sprinkle salt on both sides of the beef.
Heat the beef for 5 minutes.
Once sear from both sides, transfer it to the cooling rack.
Empty any oil left inside Ninja Foodi pot.
Now add beef broth, pepper, and sage to the pot and bring it to boil.
Add beef back and close the hood.
Adjust pressure to High and cook for 60 minutes.
Afterward, do a quick steam release.
Open the lid and add mushrooms and carrots.
Press bake and roast and cook for 20 minutes at 400 degrees F.
Once done, serve and enjoy.

Nutrition Facts

Servings: 6
Amount per serving
Calories   619
% Daily Value*
Total Fat 28.6g   37%
Saturated Fat 8.8g 44%
Cholesterol 229mg   76%
Sodium 492mg   21%
Total Carbohydrate 8g   3%
Dietary Fiber 2.7g 10%
Total Sugars 4.5g
Protein 78.2g

Roast Chicken in Ninja Foodi

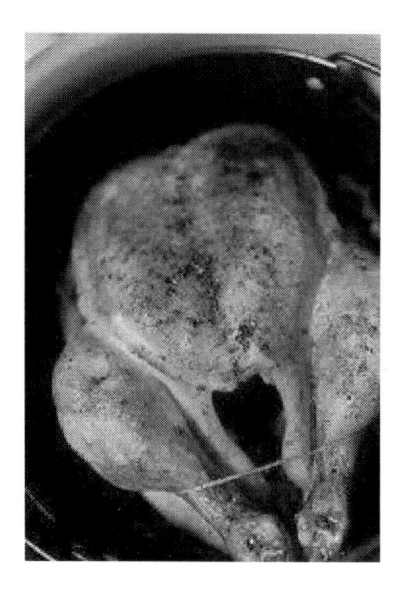

Cooking Time: 40 Minutes
Yield: 8 Servings

Ingredients

4 pounds of chicken
Salt and pepper, to taste
2 tablespoons of butter
1 tablespoon of paprika, (can use smoked paprika if you wish)
1 tablespoon garlic powder
1/2 teaspoon onion powder
2 teaspoon of seasoned salt
1 cup of water

Ingredients of Butter Sauce

4 tablespoons of butter
1/2 teaspoon of garlic powder
Salt and black pepper, to taste

Directions

Mix butter sauce ingredient in a bowl and then microwave for 20 seconds.
Wash and pat dry the chicken.
Put some water in the Ninja Foodi grill.
Next rub the chicken with salt, black pepper, butter, paprika, garlic powder, onion powder, and seasoned salt.
Set the Cook & Crisp Basket inside the unit.
Place chicken in the basket.
Seal the unit by assembling the pressure lid.
Select PRESSURE and set to high for 15 minutes.
When time completes, allow to natural release for 15 minutes.
Next, remove the lid and brush the chicken with basting butter.
Again close the unit hood and press the roast/bake.
Adjust temperate to 400 degrees Fahrenheit for 25 minutes.
Let chicken rest for 5-10 minutes.
Once the internal temperature reaches 165 degrees Fahrenheit it done, serve.

Nutrition Facts

Servings: 8
Amount per serving
Calories   425
% Daily Value*
Total Fat 15.6g   20%
Saturated Fat 7.4g   37%
Cholesterol 198mg   66%
Sodium 586mg   25%
Total Carbohydrate 1.4g   1%
Dietary Fiber 0.4g   2%
Total Sugars 0.4g
Protein 66.2g

Roasted Artichokes

Cooking Time: 20 Minutes
Yield: 3 Servings

Ingredients

3 artichokes large
1/3 cup tamari sauce
3 lemons, juiced
4 teaspoon of minced garlic
1/3 cup olive oil or broth
1 cup of vegetable broth

Directions

Cut the bottom stem of the artichoke and then cut the leaves off the vegetables.
Put the artichoke inside the Ninja Foodi.
Close the hood of the Ninja Foodi grill.
Set the Ninja Foodi grill on bake/roast for five minutes.
After 3 minutes open the hood of the unit and move the artichoke so it cooks evenly.
Roast the artichokes for 10-15 minutes. Once done, serve.

Nutrition Facts

Servings: 3
Amount per serving
Calories   318
% Daily Value*
Total Fat 23.3g   30%
Saturated Fat 3.4g 17%
Cholesterol 0mg   0%
Sodium 1749mg   76%
Total Carbohydrate 25.3g   9%
Dietary Fiber 10.6g 38%
Total Sugars 3.7g
Protein 10.3g

Salmon with Apricot Sauce

Cooking Time: 20 Minutes
Yield: 4 Servings

Ingredients

1/4 cup apricot preserves
2 teaspoons of country Dijon-style mustard
2 pounds of salmon, fillets
Salt and pepper
6 ounces of balsamic glaze
2 cup water for steaming in Ninja

Directions

Take a small bowl, and mix apricot preserves, mustard, salt, pepper, balsamic glaze.
Marinate the salmon in the glaze.
Pour your 2 cups of water inside the Ninja Foodi.
And place the rack inside it.
Cover rack with aluminum foil.
Place marinated fillet on the rack.
Press the bake/roast button by closing the hood.
Press Roast at 100 degrees F for 15 minutes.
Once done shut down the unit and uncover the fish.
Roast for 5 more minutes.

Nutrition Facts

Servings: 4
Amount per serving
Calories   1013
% Daily Value*
Total Fat 47g   60%
Saturated Fat 7.3g 36%
Cholesterol 235mg   78%
Sodium 1642mg   71%
Total Carbohydrate 50.4g   18%
Dietary Fiber 12.1g 43%
Total Sugars 28.2g
Protein 102.6g

Vegetable Egg Omelet

Cooking Time: 30 Minutes
Yield: 6 Servings

Ingredients

2 tablespoons of canola oil
1 pound of breakfast sausage
2 medium russet potato, grated
1 teaspoon of sea salt divided
1 teaspoon black pepper divided
8 large eggs
2 cups cheese shredded

Directions

Preheat the grill by pressing the Ninja Foodi bake/roast button.
Set a timer to 5 minutes at 315 degrees F.
In a mixing bowl, whisk eggs, and then add oil, sausage, russet potatoes, salt, black pepper, and cheese.
Generously grease the bottom of the Ninja Foodi baking pan with canola oil spray.
Pour the egg mixture into the pan and place pan on to the rack.
Put the rack inside the Ninja Foodi and close the hood.
Set bake/roast to 300 degrees for 30 minutes.
Once done, serve.

Nutrition Facts

Servings: 6
Amount per serving
Calories   641
% Daily Value*
Total Fat 45.4g   58%
Saturated Fat 17.3g   86%
Cholesterol 351mg   117%
Sodium 907mg   39%
Total Carbohydrate 22.4g   8%
Dietary Fiber 2.3g 8%
Total Sugars 1.8g
Protein 35.1g

Roasted Chicken Drumsticks

Cooking Time: 35 Minutes
Yield: 6 Servings

Ingredients

3 pounds of chicken drumsticks
3 Garlic cloves
4 tbsp Herbs, fresh
4 tbsp Onion powder
1 tsp Bouillon powder
1/2 teaspoon Cayenne pepper
1 teaspoon Paprika, smoked
Salt and black pepper, to taste
1 teaspoon White pepper
1/3 cup Canola oil

Directions

Rinse and pat dry the chicken legs with a paper towel.
In a small bowl and mix all the listed ingredients in it.
Rub the legs generously with the rub.
Place chicken in cook and crisp basket.
Place the basket inside the Ninja Foodi.
Lock the lid and pressure cook for 20 minutes for 10 minutes.
Release the pressure for 15 minutes naturally.
Baste the chicken with more canola oil.
Close the crisping lid.
Select roast and set time to 15 minutes at 375degreess.
Once done, serve and enjoy.

Nutrition Facts

Servings: 6
Amount per serving
Calories   512
% Daily Value*
Total Fat 25.2g   32%
Saturated Fat 4.3g 22%
Cholesterol 200mg   67%
Sodium 187mg   8%
Total Carbohydrate 5g   2%
Dietary Fiber 0.8g 3%
Total Sugars 1.7g
Protein 63.1g

Spaghetti Squash

Cooking Time: 15 Minutes
Yield: 4 Servings

Ingredients

2 pounds of spaghetti squash
Salt and black pepper
Canola oil spray, for greasing

Directions

Pierce the squash using fork or knife.
Season it with salt and black pepper.
Coat it with canola oil spray.
Put squash inside the Ninja Foodi.
Set the Ninja Foodi grill on bake/roast for five minutes.
After 5 minutes, open the hood of the unit and move the squash.
Cook the squash for 10 more minutes.

Nutrition Facts

Servings: 4
Amount per serving
Calories   72
% Daily Value*
Total Fat 1.4g   2%
Saturated Fat 0.3g 1%
Cholesterol 0mg   0%
Sodium 39mg   2%
Total Carbohydrate 15.7g   6%
Dietary Fiber 0g   0%
Total Sugars 0g
Protein 1.5g

Homemade Biscuits in Ninja Foodi

Cooking Time: 12 Minutes
Yield: 6 Servings

Ingredients

2.5 cups flour all-purpose, chilled
Pinch of sea salt
1 tablespoon baking powder
2 tablespoons granulated white sugar
8 tablespoons butter salted
1/3 cup Greek yogurt plain, whole fat, unsweetened
1/3 cup water

Directions

Turn on the bake function of the Ninja Foodi.
Set the timer to 20 minutes at 375 degrees F for preheating.
Mix flour, baking soda, salt, sugar in a large mixing bowl.
Add butter to the bowl and mix with the flour until coarse texture achieved
Make a hole in the middle of the butter-flour mixture.
Pour Greek yogurt and water, mix well to make the dough
Dump this mixture on to a floured flat surface
Knit it a few times
Each time it's been knitted, make the square bigger
Now roll it flat
Use a biscuit cutter to cut the biscuits. Press down and twist to cut the biscuits
Cut as many biscuits as you want to prepare
Only 6-8 will fit in the Ninja Foodi
Layer the biscuits on to Ninja Foodi basket.
Put the basket into the inner pot.
Press the Roast button.
Set temperate to 375 degrees for 12 minutes.
Once done, serve.

Nutrition Facts

Servings: 6
Amount per serving
Calories   313
% Daily Value*
Total Fat 21.5g   28%
Saturated Fat 4.5g 23%
Cholesterol 0mg   0%
Sodium 241mg   10%
Total Carbohydrate 21.7g   8%
Dietary Fiber 3g   11%
Total Sugars 7.4g
Protein 13.2g

Blueberry Cake

Cooking Time: 32 Minutes
Yield: 4 Servings

Ingredients

2 cups almond flour
2 teaspoons baking soda
1/4 teaspoon salt
1/2 cup butter, softened
3/4 cup stevia
2 eggs
3/4 cup coconut milk
6 ounces of fresh blueberries

Directions

Mix butter, salt, stevia, and baking soda in a large mixing bowl.
Whisk well with hand beater.
Once fluffy, add flour, milk, and fresh blueberries.
Then add the whisked eggs, mix the ingredients into a smooth batter.
Spoon the mixture to an oil greased small loaf pan.
Place the pan on the wire rack.
Put the rack inside Ninja Foodi.
Shut the unit and turn on the bake function.
Set temperate to 325 degrees F for 32 minutes.
Once done, serve.

Nutrition Facts

Servings: 4
Amount per serving
Calories   447
% Daily Value*
Total Fat 42.7g   55%
Saturated Fat 25.3g   126%
Cholesterol 143mg   48%
Sodium 983mg   43%
Total Carbohydrate 11.8g   4%
Dietary Fiber 3.5g   13%
Total Sugars 5.9g
Protein 7.4g

Lemongrass and Coconut Chicken

Cooking Time: 30 Minutes
Yield: 2 Servings

Ingredients

2 pounds of chicken legs
1/4 cup of Lemongrass
1/2 cup of coconut
Salt, to taste
Black pepper, to taste
2 teaspoon of lemon juice
1 teaspoon of red chili flakes

Directions

Take a bowl and mix lemon juice, lemongrass, coconut, red chili flakes, salt, black paper, and water.
Pour the liquid in the zip lock bag.
Roasting basket.
Put the chicken inside the bag.
Marinate it for a few hours.
Pour the liquid and chicken in the roasting basket.
Place basket inside Ninja Foodi
Put pressure lid on.
Pressure cook on high for 22 minutes.
Once done, take off the pressure lid, by releasing pressure naturally of 15 minutes.
Discard lemongrass and close the hood of Ninja Foodi.
Press roast and cook for 10 minutes at 400 degrees f.
Serve and enjoy with liquid collected at the bottom.

Nutrition Facts

Servings: 2
Amount per serving
Calories   942
% Daily Value*
Total Fat 40.4g   52%
Saturated Fat 15.2g   76%
Cholesterol 404mg   135%
Sodium 473mg   21%
Total Carbohydrate 5.3g 2%
Dietary Fiber 1.8g 7%
Total Sugars 1.4g
Protein 132.1g

Roasted Cauliflower

Cooking Time: 20 Minutes
Yield: 4 Servings

Ingredients

1 small cauliflower, florets
Salt and black pepper, to taste
1/3 cup olive oil

Directions

Cut the bottom stem of the cauliflower and cut into florets.
Sprinkle salt and black pepper on top and rub oil all around.
Put the cauliflower inside the Ninja Foodi.
Close the hood of the Ninja Foodi grill.
Set the Ninja Foodi grill on bake/roast for five minutes.
After 3 minutes open the hood of the unit and move the artichoke so it cooks evenly.
Roast the artichokes for 15 minutes.
Once done, serve.

Nutrition Facts

Servings: 4
Amount per serving
Calories   161
% Daily Value*
Total Fat 16.9g   22%
Saturated Fat 2.4g 12%
Cholesterol 0mg   0%
Sodium 20mg   1%
Total Carbohydrate 3.5g 1%
Dietary Fiber 1.7g 6%
Total Sugars 1.6g
Protein 1.3g

Chapter No 6:21 Days Meal Plan

The only thing that is important to create a meal plan is planning and budget, still it is not a complex process and very easy to create, once you have the idea and recipes readily available. The main focus should be on the mission of buying and purchasing effectively the food items that helps produce recipes idea for 21 days. Grab the grocery bag; fill the food cart by going straight to the food section to buy items for the specific week. Don't lose time and waste money on the items that derail us from the track like little things on sale, etc.

The first step is to create a grocery list for the specific week.
Make sure you buy organic, whole, and most healthy food items out in the market.
Look at the recipe for a particle day and prepare all the necessary ingredients you needed.
Keep all the things in the budget.
Be fast, effective and efficient.

The shopping list is important for cooking for a specific day. It is important to read the food label carefully when buying products.

When you are going for shopping you need to have a very good idea of recipe ingredients. Only buy new items when your refrigerator is out of stock. Some items are usually in sale in bulk, buying such items can save your money, time, and help in meal prep ideas in the long run. If you are preparing a meal rather than a normal routine and for a special occasion than you need time to set it on the table. If you are thinking to cook frozen food items then it needed to be defrosted and cook it properly. If a day is needed to defrost then it should be done earlier, so the time should not be wasted.

Take the time to purchase accessories that needed for recipe preparation. It will make cooking easier in the long run.

Week 1

Week 1	Saturday	Sunday	Monday	Tuesday	Wednesday	Thursday	Friday
Breakfast	Vegetable Egg Omelet	Breakfast Stuffed Peppers	Ninja Foodi Baked Gluten-Free Oatmeal	Mushroom and Egg Omelet	Hash Brown	Vegetable Egg Omelet	Air Fryer Breakfast Frittata
Lunch	Roast Chicken in Ninja Foodi	Grilled Chicken Legs in Ninja Foodi	Ninja Foodi Prime Rib	Wings Recipe	Air Fryer Steak Bites & Mushrooms	Air Fried Lamb Chops	Roasted Artichokes
Dinner	Spaghetti Squash	Tri-Tip Roast In Ninja Foodi	Ninja Foodi Rosemary Roast and Potatoes	Teriyaki Salmon	Roasted Chicken Drumsticks	Teriyaki Salmon	Air Fryer Chicken Breast
Snack	Chocolate Chip Cookie Cake	Dehydrated Pineapple	Dehydrated Squash	Cajun Seasoned Shrimp	Crispy Air Fryer Chickpeas	Dehydrating Sweet Potato In Ninja Foodi	Dehydrating Sweet Potato In Ninja Foodi

Week 2

Week2	Saturday	Sunday	Monday	Tuesday	Wednesday	Thursday	Friday
Breakfast	Delicious Donuts in Ninja Foodi Grill	Monkey Bread	Ninja Foodi Apple Dump Cake	Baked Western Omelet	Vegetable Egg Omelet	Monkey bread	Monkey Bread
Lunch	Beef Chuck Roast with Root Vegetables	Frozen Barbecue Chicken Breasts	Tri-Tip Roast In Ninja Foodi	Ninja Foodi Pumpkin Bread	Roasted Chicken Drumsticks	Air-Fryer Eggplant Fries	Roasted Chicken Drumsticks
Dinner	Ninja Foodi Grill Marinated Steak	Grilled Salmon	Air Fryer Rib-Eye Steak	Air Fryer Chicken Breast	Pork Roast	BBQ Ribs	Ninja Foodi Roast Chicken
Snack	Grilled Broccoli	Grilled Plantains	Dehydrated Watermelons	Dehydrated bananas	Dehydrating Sweet Potato In Ninja Foodi	Citrus Crisps	Dehydrated Mangoes

Week 3

Week3	Saturday	Sunday	Monday	Tuesday	Wednesday	Thursday	Friday
Breakfast	Air Fryer Breakfast Frittata	Cheesy Egg Bake	Ninja Foodi Baked Pumpkin Oatmeal	Ninja Foodi Lemon Cream Cheese Dump Cake	Baked Western Omelet	Walnuts and Raspberries Cake	Monkey Bread
Lunch	Air Fryer Chicken Fajita Tacos	Ninja Foodi Turkey Breast	Bake Potatoes In Ninja Foodi Grill	Baked Fish in Ninja Foodi	Herbed Chicken	Pork Roast	Salmon with Apricot Sauce
Dinner		Air Fried Lamb Chops	Air Fried Teriyaki Chicken	Fish and Grits	Ninja Foodi Pressure Cooker Pot Roast Recipe	Air Fryer Ninja Foodi Eggplant	Teriyaki Salmon
Snack	Cajun Seasoned Shrimp	Dehydrated Pineapple	Air Fryer Acorn Squash	Grilled Broccoli	Roasted Artichokes	Ninja Foodi French Fries	Crispy Air Fryer Chickpeas

Conclusion

I hope the basic aim of this cookbook is achieved and it helps teach the beginner and Ninja Foodi Smart XL Indoor Grill users how to effectively use and set up this appliance and how to create some mouth-watering meal consistently. The skill of cooking with Ninja Foodi Smart XL Indoor Grill lies in practicing and using the right time and temperature for specific food item prepared by a different function of Ninja Foodi Smart XL Indoor Grill.

After reading the book, you will have very good ideas on how to prepare a healthy meal, as this book covers about 100 healthy meals, low in fat and high in protein.

Made in the USA
Middletown, DE
14 December 2020